A Foraging Vacation

by Raquel Boehmer
illustrations by Anne Kilham

Down East BOOKS
CAMDEN, MAINE

A Foraging Vacation

Library of Congress Catalog Card No. 82-71091
ISBN 0-89272-139-1
Design: Anne Kilham
Composition: The Offset House, S. Burlington, Vt.
Manufactured in the United States of America

Down East Books / *Camden, Maine*

Acknowledgments

This book is dedicated to Bill Legere, who started this all, and to my trusting, wonderful family.

Special thanks to the many people who have influenced and helped me in this work. Very high amongst them are:

Maine Public Broadcasting folk, George Putz, Laurie Cooper, Marilis and Hank Hornidge, Paul Harris, Phil Conkling, Barry Timpson, Robert Semple, Billy Payne, Captains Sherm and Alfred Stanley, Teco Slagboom, Jaqueline Davenport and my gentle editor Karin Womer. And, of course, the late Euell Gibbons, whose infectious spirit lives on.

The shore is an ancient world, for as long as there has been an earth and sea there has been this place of the meeting of land and water. Yet it is a world that keeps alive the sense of continuing creation and of the relentless drive of life. Each time that I enter it, I gain some new awareness of its beauty and its deeper meanings, sensing that intricate fabric of life by which one creature is linked with another, and each with its surroundings.

Rachel Carson
from *The Edge of the Sea*

Contents

Introduction 1

Notes on Tides and Boating 3

Foraging 4–41

- Zone I Sea Water (fin fish, crab) 5
- Zone II Intertidal Land (shellfish, seaweeds) 15
- Zone III The Shoreline 24
  - Spring and Early Summer (greens, beach peas, strawberries) 25
  - Summer (greens, beach peas, mints, berries) 32
  - Late Summer and Autumn (greens, sea rocket, beach peas) 38

Recipes 43–109

- Zone I Sea Water 45
- Zone II Intertidal Land 73
- Zone III The Shoreline 94

Items to Bring Along 111

Meal Accompaniments 114

Some Final Thoughts 119

Resources and State Agencies 120

Bibliography 121

Index 122

Index 123

Introduction

A VACATION TRIP downeast can turn into a love affair with the varied coast of Maine. Some people discover the joys of her convoluted coastline and offshore islands in sail or power boats. Others, who camp in her woods or stay in cottages or motels, experience her timeless shore and forests in cars, on foot, and in small boats. Maine's coast offers abundant examples of unspoiled beauty and the natural order. They make their impressions on us, giving hope, joy, and even courage, with which to truly live our lives.

The societal pressures we experience in our day-to-day lives require rapid change and extraordinary flexibility. It is with pure delight that we witness and participate in nature's cycles as they unfold in their ordained patterns: the plants and animals that come and go with the seasons, the tides, moons, and the earth's orbit. The constancy and order of this cyclical renewal offers comfort and hope.

Nature's patterns exist, however, not just to be studied; they exist to be mingled with. Foraging — a means of living off the offerings of sea and land — takes us away from the processed and prepackaged world we live in. It increases our interest in nature, makes us more observant, and teaches us how things grow and interrelate. Foraging is an especially good family experience, and as we gather our sustenance, we can teach our children respect for the beauty and bounty of nature in a gentle and loving way. Foraging is a conscious way of touching life.

The intent of this handbook is to show the beginner how to forage along Maine's coast. It does not attempt to be a complete guide to all the edibles of this rich habitat; rather, it should serve as a basic introduction to foraging — and, I hope, as an inspiration to continue discovering wild foods. The first section divides the seaside into three separate zones — sea water, intertidal land, and shoreline — and gives basic identification and gathering information on the various plant and sea life easily found there. These plants and animals can furnish the majority of ingredients for your meals, or they can be gathered and prepared as special additions to your menu.

Three popular seafoods — lobsters, clams, and scallops — have been omitted from the foraging instructions, but are included in the recipe section. They can be purchased at fish wharves, cooperatives, and markets, from the Maine fishermen whose livelihood they represent.

Actually, catching lobsters and scallops requires intricate apparatus and a state license, and those who earn their living from these shellfish vigorously guard their territories. If foraging a "mess o' clams" is essential to your idea of a Maine vacation, check first with the local marine patrol officer to see if local digging permits are required and to check on whether the clam flats are polluted or contaminated by Red Tide. Restrict your digging to areas around the edges of big rocks and ledges, thus avoiding the areas harvested by commercial clamdiggers.

The second section of this book consists of delicious and varied recipes for foraged foods. The methods are familiar, making it easy to substitute these gathered items for the standard fare.

Vacations can be times when we consciously decide to do things out of the ordinary rhythms of our daily lives. They can be times to relax, but they can also be times in which to gather energy from new impressions. If you have already chosen to spend your vacation in exquisitely beautiful coastal Maine, you can find new rhythms and impressions by making foraging a focus of your vacation.

For more information, be certain to peruse the suggested reading list at the end of the book.

An invitation to readers: Comments, ideas, and inquiries will be gratefully accepted. Address correspondence to: Raquel Boehmer
c/o Down East Books
P.O. Box 679
Camden, Maine 04843

Notes on Tides and Boating

TIDES ARE AN ESSENTIAL consideration if you're planning to forage along the coast of Maine. Consult a tide calendar to determine the best conditions for gathering various foods from the intertidal land (Zone III). Tide calendars are generally available in boatyards, ship chandleries, coastal bookstores, and hardware stores. Day-to-day information on tides is available in coastal newspapers.

The tide reaches its highest and lowest point, not, as many believe, when the moon is directly overhead, but when the moon is full or new. When the tidal range between high and low water is greatest, it's called the *spring* or *moon* tide.

Neap tide, its opposite, occurs during the first and third quarters of the moon's phases, when the difference between high and low water is smallest. Watch for the spring or moon tide as the maximum amount of intertidal land is exposed at this time, making it easy to forage for seafood.

By using a tide calendar, you can predict the time and height of high and low waters by registering the difference between them each day of the month.

Always keep the tides in mind when you're in a small boat. Tide differentials range from 9½ to 18 feet, west to east along Maine's coast. If you come ashore, whether on an island or along the coast, pull up your boat far enough from the water's edge to prevent its washing out to sea. When tying a boat up at a dock or wharf, leave a long enough line so that your boat will not be left hanging in mid-air when the tide recedes.

When foraging or spending time on the water in a small boat, use a bit of caution in choosing the day and planning the distance you'll travel. Fog is a serious summer condition on coastal waters; particularly in the late afternoons. It comes on quickly and a boat can get lost in a matter of minutes. If fog is predicted, stay close to familiar shoreline.

Note: For a few suggestions on where a small boat might be rented, consult the resources section at the back of the book.

Section I — Foraging

Zone I
Sea Water (Coastal)

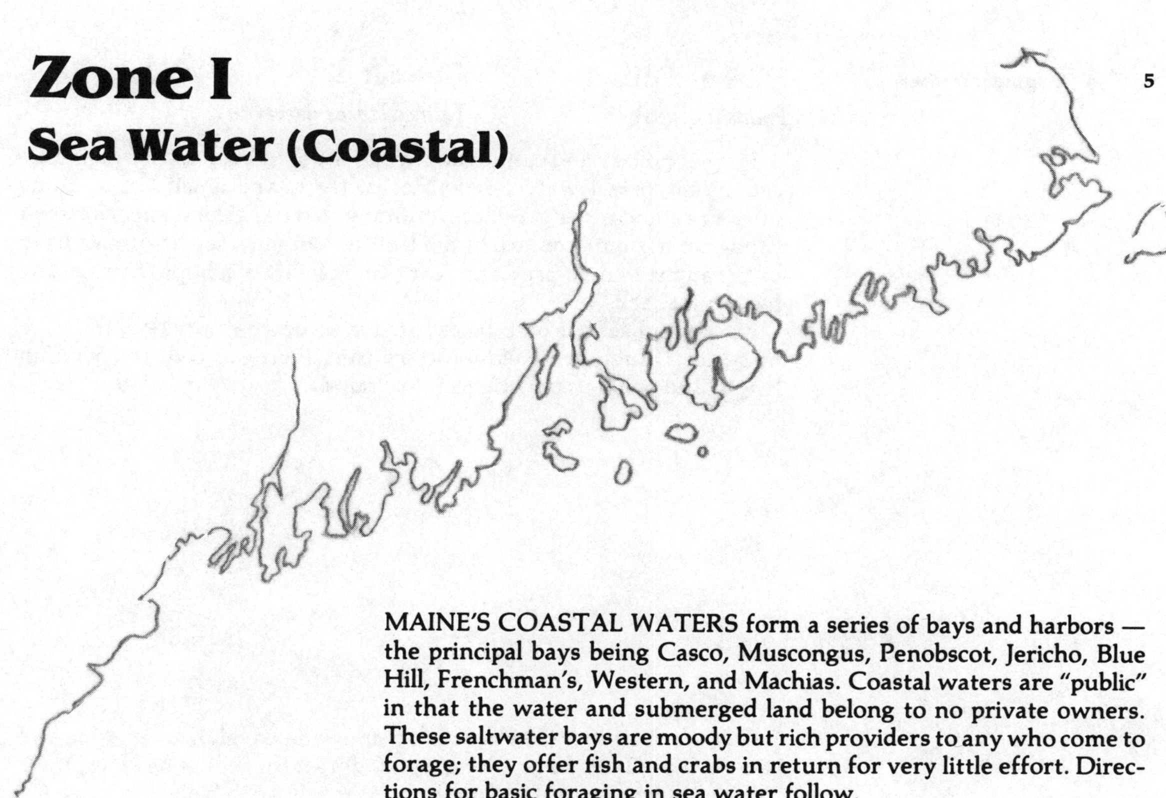

MAINE'S COASTAL WATERS form a series of bays and harbors — the principal bays being Casco, Muscongus, Penobscot, Jericho, Blue Hill, Frenchman's, Western, and Machias. Coastal waters are "public" in that the water and submerged land belong to no private owners. These saltwater bays are moody but rich providers to any who come to forage; they offer fish and crabs in return for very little effort. Directions for basic foraging in sea water follow.

Harbor Pollack
Pollachius virens

Cunner
Tautogolabrus adspersus

Harbor pollack and cunner are two of the species of fin fish generally caught in coastal waters from docks, piers, and small boats. Some people prefer cunner to pollack, claiming that its flavor is superior even though it has more bones. In the last few seasons, fewer cunner have been caught than in previous years; one can always hope they are due for a comeback.

Harbor pollack are blue-black in color, somewhat speckled, and have no scales. Caught in shallow waters, they average a foot and a half in length and weigh from one to four pounds.

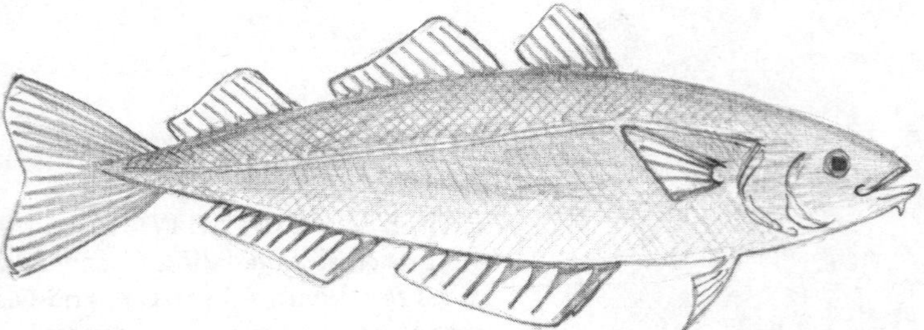

Cunner are generally about a foot long and weigh between one and two pounds. They have a long, spiny dorsal fin that runs along their topsides. They are mainly brown, with a yellowish belly.

Before you try your hand at fishing for either type, you will need a bit of fishing gear. If you have a casting rod, fit it with some clear monofilament line, 10- to 12-pound test. A drop or hand line can also be used. You will need to fasten one or two small sinkers to the line, depending on how fast you want your line to go down, and a hook or lure. A favorite hook for cunner or pollack is called a diamond jig.

You will also need a sharp knife and a bucket to hold some sea water and the fish as they are caught. As for bait, if you use a diamond jig, its shiny surface is usually sufficient to attract the fish. If you want to use live bait, periwinkles work well. Nightcrawlers, the standard bait, are always good to use, as are canned clams and pieces of pork rind. But since this is a seacoast foraging adventure, the jig and periwinkles seem more appropriate.

The best time for fishing is when the mood strikes, although some say that fishing is best on an incoming tide. If there is a noticeable current in the water, use it to your advantage if you're casting. Once

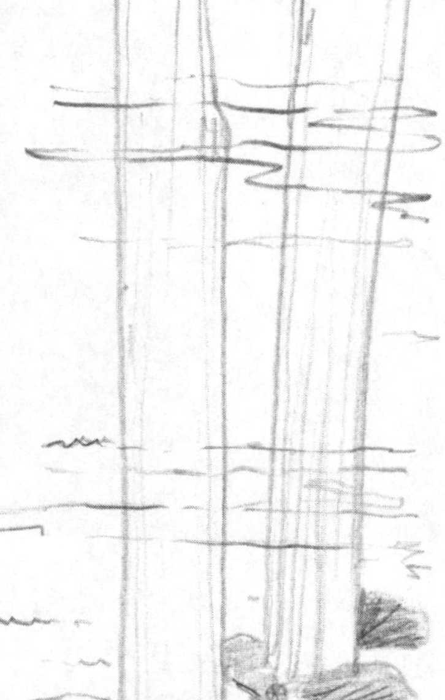

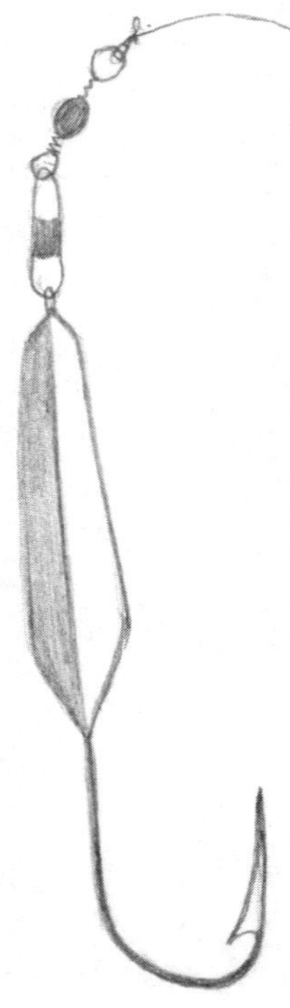

you've cast out, "jig" the line with a jerking motion and allow the slack you have pulled off the reel to pay out in the direction of the current. The object is to get the jig almost to the bottom — maybe even hitting the bottom — then reel in or come up a bit.

If your jig should get fetched up on the bottom, pay out more line, let the tide take it a bit, and then pull up. If that does not work, try pulling from the opposite direction. If you are in a boat, secure your rod or line and move up-tide. If you are fishing from a wharf, work down a ways to change the angle of your line. Jigs are expensive, so you don't want to lose them.

With a free line, begin to jig upward, reeling back a bit of line with each little jerk and keeping the jig in motion. The advantage of a rod and reel is that you can work your line horizontally, increasing your chances of "foul snatching" a fish, i.e. catching a fish by snagging it in the flesh even if it hasn't taken the hook in its mouth. Using a fishing rod also allows you to cover a broader area of sea bottom, where the fish may be schooling.

When you have caught your first fish, take it from the jig hook and slit its belly with your knife. Cut off a small sliver of meat with skin on one side and attach it to the hook. The skin's toughness helps the piece stay on the hook. This bit of meat will attract more of the same fish; it adds the element of smell to the flash or gleam of the diamond jig. Use another bit of flesh whenever one piece falls off the hook.

As you catch your fish, remove them from the jig hook and place them in a bucket of cool sea water, out of the sun. With luck, and a bit of skill, your bucket will fill steadily!

Recipes for harbor pollack and cunner follow in the recipe section.

Atlantic Mackerel

Scomber scombrus

Atlantic mackerel, like cunner and harbor pollack, are also scaleless fin fish and very spiny. They are related to tuna and bluefish. The body of a mackerel is sleek and streamlined, almost spindle shaped, and ends in a deeply forked tail. Their color shades from iridescent green to blue, and they have black horizontal striping along the sides which lightens to a silver belly. They measure from a foot to a foot and a half in length and generally weigh between 1¼ and 2 pounds. Young mackerel called tinker are slightly smaller but have the same general appearance as the adult Atlantic mackerel.

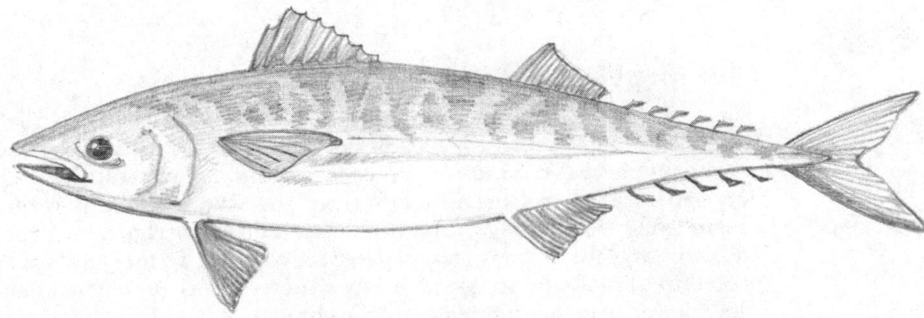

The method for catching mackerel does not differ substantially from that for harbor pollack and cunner. The diamond jig, sometimes called a mackerel jig, is all you need to use for bait. Some people like to use yoked jigs which have three jigs hung together.

Mackerel, unlike other fish, can be seen in the water as they school close to the surface. If you are in a boat, stay on the edge of one of these teeming schools to avoid startling the fish. When mackerel are running (the peak season is generally July and August) you might catch some from a dock, but they are seldom that close to shore.

Using the same jigging action described before, jerk the lure to attract or foul snatch the fish. When mackerel are about, you may think you are breaking all sorts of records. Tales of catching one fish per minute are not rare. Be certain to bring in enough to give you leftovers. Recipes using mackerel follow in the recipe section.

Cleaning Fish

In order to live off the sea you need to know how to clean and fillet fish. Some people relish the idea of doing everything for themselves and enjoy the basic hands-on procedures. But for others, the gulf between foraged and fished foods from the wild and the portion-controlled, kitchen-ready packet is a difficult one to bridge. However, once caught, your fish must be prepared for cooking. To that end, some procedures follow. As one garners experience, the task becomes easier, allowing for personal refinements in technique.

When cleaning small bony fish such as harbor pollack or cunner, it is better not to fillet them. The following method for cleaning small fish will give you a broad piece of fish with more meat than a fillet. Some of the thin-rayed bones will be cut off with the meat, but the bones of these fish are actually considered soft and chewable.

Place the fish on its side, on a board, and using a filleting knife (or one with a sharp, fairly long blade) make a downward cut behind the gill, penetrating only halfway through. Keeping the knife in the same cut, draw it down to the stomach area and back to the tail. The body cavity will be fully opened so you can grasp all the entrails and pull them out in one motion; discard these. Lay the fish open against the board; take the knife and proceed to make long cuts down both sides of the backbone. Next, cut through the backbone at the top (head end) and lift up, taking the whole backbone out, including the tail. Sever the head from the body. (Note: save the heads of any fish you clean if you plan to catch crabs.) Some bones will be left in the meat using this method, but the backbone will be gone and the remaining bones will soften as they cook. If you want to cut them away, bend back the lower part of the fish's side and cut out most of these little rayed bones by getting your knife against them and drawing it close to the bones — in effect, peeling them away. By this method you have one double-spread piece rather than two very small fillets. If desired, the larger pieces can be cut in half.

Rinse the fish in a bucket of cold sea water, or in some heavily salted fresh water. If you must use fresh water alone, do not soak the fish longer than is absolutely necessary, as fresh water will soften the fish's texture. Refrigerate the fish or keep them in a cooler until you are ready to use them.

Filleting

If you're going to fillet your fish, they needn't be cleaned or deheaded. Using a knife with a sharp point, insert it into the fish just behind the gills, on either side of the backbone. Cut a line back to the tail section, following the backbone and trying not to cut into it. Be aware of what your knife is touching and respond to those discernible differences of texture between flesh and bone. Make a cut from the gill downward. Insert the blade of the knife in the backbone cut and peel away the fillet, proceeding from the top of the fish downward. When the meat is clear of most of the rayed bones (thin ribs), separate it from the body.

Place the fillet skin side down on a board, securing the piece by bearing down with your fingertips (and even nails) on the skin only. Now, with the knife, detach the skin from the flesh by running the blade as close to the skin as possible, pulling the knife firmly but with a slight sawing action, if needed. This will produce a small boneless and skinless piece of fish: the fillet. Repeat this procedure with the other side.

Mackerel can be filleted and cleaned in this manner, but there is another method which is easy and especially well suited to this fleshy fish. Holding the fish down on a board by its head, and with fingers right in the gill slit for steadying, take a fillet knife and slice or skim the fillet off horizontally — starting just behind the gill. Continue to pull your knife back to the tail, staying as close to the backbone as possible. This procedure will give you a practically boneless fillet with an iridescent, scaleless, edible skin on one side. Plunge each mackerel fillet into a bucket of cold sea water, or a prepared solution of well-salted fresh water. The fillets will now "bleed out" and you may leave them in the cold salted water until you're ready to cook them, even overnight.

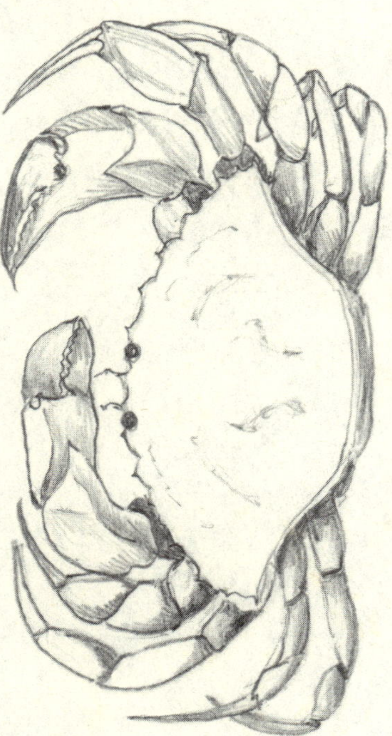

Rock Crab

Cancer irroratus

Crabmeat is probably one of the most delectable taste treats available to the forager — and it is easy to obtain. Crabs can be collected on foot, at low tide, from under or between rocks. It is advisable to wear boots, old sneakers, or flip-flops for this sort of wading, since there may be barnacles, broken glass, and sharp shells under foot. Crabs can also be fished from a boat in shallow clear water using a baited line or hook. Adult crabs generally measure about 3" by 4", have a yellowish back mottled with brown, and look just as you would expect a crab to look.

If you wish to catch crabs with your hands, be careful of their large front pincher claws; grasp them by a back leg, or grab the carapace (back) itself. Although quick and agile, they cannot reach your fingers while you are holding them in this manner. Sometimes you can use your dip net and scoop crabs up. Unless you manage to sneak up on them in their darker hideouts in crevices, you will be surprised at how swiftly they can scamper away.

From a boat, a good way to catch crabs is to use a line and hook, with a fish head for bait. If you don't have a hook, you can just string the head on a line. Lower the bait until it is a few inches off the bottom. If the water is clear and fairly shallow, you will be able to see when crabs have begun to feed on the fish head. Now raise the hook very gently so that you do not cause them to lose their hold on the bait. Place your dip net under the crab as soon as you can, or it may well release its hold and fall back into the water before you've landed it.

Once collected, steam or boil the crabs in a pot with only a few inches of boiling water for 5 to 10 minutes once the water begins to steam again. You can add a bayberry leaf or two (Zone III) and some pepper, seafood seasoning, and a handful of rockweed (Zone II). Once they've cooked, immediately chill the crabs by pouring very cold water over them; this will aid in picking out the meat.

Since the major part of the crabmeat is taken from the front claws (although there is meat in the body cavity), some fishermen reduce the volume of crabs to be boiled by harvesting only the large front claws. They pull off the front claws from live crabs, then return the crabs to the sea, where they regenerate the lost limbs. (Cook claws for five minutes only, following the directions given above. Do not be surprised by involuntary reflex action in the claws while they are being steamed.)

In any event, after such cooking and chilling, use a nut or seafood cracker and break open the shell of each of the three sections of the crab's claw leg. With a nut pick or the thin handle of a teaspoon remove the white and delicate meat. Be aware of a stiff membrane that should be separated from the flesh of each pincher in the large first section. It is a good practice to keep dipping your fingers into clear water to remove any chips of shell that might get into the meat pile. Allow one hour of picking-out time to prepare 1 cup of clear, sweet crabmeat.

Recipes can be found in the recipe section of this book.

Zone II
Intertidal Land

PERHAPS BECAUSE OF ITS constantly changing shape, the intertidal zone legally belongs to no private landowners and is, therefore, open territory for foragers.

Since seaweeds and barnacles generally cover the rocks in this region, it is good to be aware of the dangers to those who tread this no man's land; always exercise caution and wear footgear.

The intertidal zone is the area between the low- and high-water mark, where earth and sea unite in a wet, but firm, stretch of sand, mud, pebbles, or rocks. It is simply teeming with life. Twice each day, the tides feed the wet land with the ocean's richness; their ebb and flow provide conditions that foster a wide variety of living organisms.

Tidepools are found in this zone. These are small bodies of water for which the tides act as a kind of slow respiration; they are covered when the tide flows and left accessible when the tide ebbs. Tidal pools often are microcosms of the larger sea, complete with plants and animals.

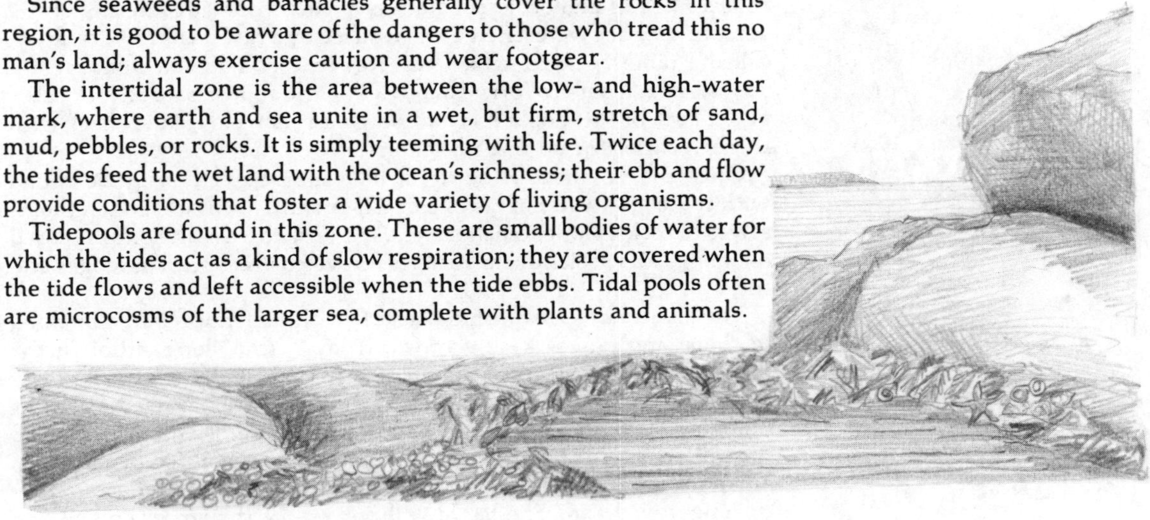

Blue Mussel

Mytilus edulis

This prolific and deliciously edible member of the mollusk family is abundant in the intertidal zone of Maine's coast. When gathering mussels, pay serious attention to the possibility of contamination. A condition known as "Red Tide" affects these creatures whose livers collect nitrates and other substances in their constant filtering of the surrounding sea water. Red Tide is caused by a tiny planktonic creature called a dinoflagellate, which secretes toxins. You can find out if a specific area is safe to forage in by calling the appropriate agency listed at the back of this book. As conditions can change rapidly, check with these agencies for up-to-date reports.

Once the go-ahead is secured, blue mussels can easily be found within the low-water areas of a beach or shore. Mussels attach themselves to rocks, pilings, anchors, etc. It is wise to leave the ones exposed on pilings and seek out those in less traveled areas such as ledges and rocks.

The mussel looks like a blue-black clam, though noticeably elongated in shape and ranges in adult form from 2" to 6" long although the tenderest and sweetest measure between 2" and 3". Its interior is pearly white with blue or violet shading, while the animal itself is bright orange. The mussel attaches to a station by means of a tough, threaded "beard" which forms a remarkably steadfast anchor. To pry it loose, grasp the larger, more curved end and then pull up and around by turning your hand. The beard will pull out of the larger end and be mostly removed. Collect about one to two dozen mussels per eater.

Scrub the outside of each shell thoroughly using a stiff scrub brush, and remove any further bits of beard that you can with a sharp knife or scissors. Rinse the mussels in fresh water with a small amount of cornmeal added to aid in their internal self-cleaning process. They will flush themselves rid of the cornmeal and any other coarse particles that might be within. Once cleaned, the mussels are ready to be cooked in any of the recipes found in the second section. They can be kept, drained, in your cooler for one or two days. If you are on a boat, these live mussels can be stored for several days in a mesh bag hung in the sea water alongside.

Periwinkles

Littorinidae

Periwinkles are the easiest creatures to forage in the intertidal zone; their presence is obvious on any beach or shoreline at low tide. You can collect quantities of these marine snails in very little time.

There are three dominant species: the smooth round periwinkle (*Littorina obstutata*) is the smallest (½″) and ranges in color from yellow, orange, or brown, to green or black, and sometimes is even striped; the rough periwinkle (*L. saxatilis*) is a bit larger (¾″), darker in color, and has a bit of a peaked top; the largest of the three, the common periwinkle (*L. littorea*) can reach 1¼″ in length and is also dark, with discernible ridges along its spire-shaped shell.

To collect these plentiful creatures, consult a tide calendar and schedule your trip to the water's edge at the hours around low tide. Wear rubber-soled shoes or boots with tread as you probably will be walking in an area where rocks are generally under water and covered with slippery seaweed. If you can locate a sandy beach with rocks on it, this will make your foraging easier. Check for periwinkles in crevices in the rocks, in and under seaweeds, and between rocks. As you walk, choose your footholds with care. Gather the largest of the available "winkles," and take only the live ones that cling to a surface with a gentle suction.

When you are ready to cook them, leave in the bits of rockweed you may have grasped and pulled off with the periwinkles; it will add flavor.

Recipes for periwinkles follow in the second section.

Sea Urchin

Strongylocentrotus drobachiensis

If this book could have one deep and far-reaching effect, it would be marvelous if it were the gastronomical discovery of the sea urchin. In general, Americans have never given this spiny, somewhat forbidding marine creature any respect. In Europe — notably in Spain, Portugal, and France — people pay money for what they consider a delicacy, while our fishermen see urchins as pests and squash them and scale them overboard. I'm sure there is a market waiting to be developed, but first, the individual palate must be educated. On to the unlikely, but possible, superstar: the green sea urchin.

The urchins available in Maine's waters are mostly green with some variation in color. They are 2" to 3" in diameter, and totally surrounded by movable radiating spines (hedgehog fashion) that measure about ½" in length. You can pick them up with your hands (wearing old cotton work gloves if you desire) and collect them from shallow water and the larger tide pools.

You will have no trouble locating the abundant sea urchin throughout the year, though midsummer to autumn is the best time to forage them. They have more egg sacs, the edible part, during this period. At low tide, and wearing footgear, walk around the rocks and you will see small greenish-purple globular creatures. Although a thing of beauty, the sea urchin appears sinister in the water and should be respected. Its spines are sharp and a puncture from one results in a stinging welt. In a bucket, collect five to ten urchins for each person.

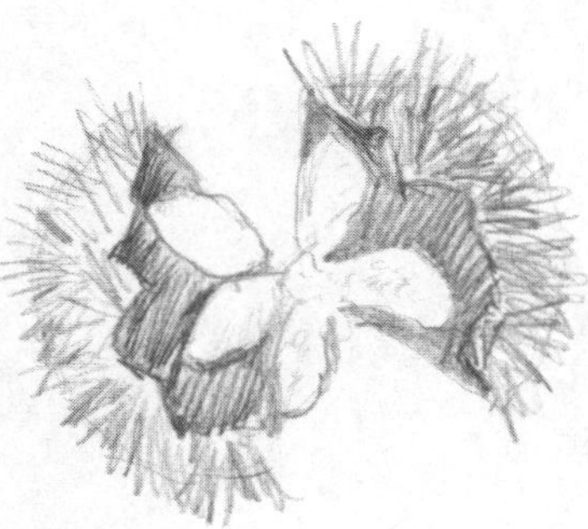

To clean them, turn one over to show its mouth and, with a lobster cracker or rock, break the shell (called the test) in two. Now you will see the five sections of orange or coral-colored roe sacs against the side opposite the mouth — most of the soft mass in the creature. Those of deep orange color are best, so use only those, if you have plenty. Remove these, place them in a bowl of cool, salted water, and discard the rest of the urchin. Gently swish the roe sacs in the water to clean them. Drain, and they are now ready to be eaten. Suggestions follow in the recipe section.

Sea Vegetables

GENERALLY, THE FIRST MENTION of eating sea vegetables — seaweeds — evokes a startled response. Those startled people are even more surprised when they learn that they have probably eaten seaweed extracts for years as stabilizers and thickeners in various foods and drugs. Not only do ice cream, dessert, dressing, sauce and drug manufacturers know the value and applications of seaweeds, but the people of Asia have long relied on seaweeds in their diets to provide essential nutrients. Seaweeds are richer in minerals, organic iodine, and potassium than any other vegetables and have high concentrations of many vitamins. In addition, they provide necessary trace elements found in sea water.

Although Maine's coastal waters offer several types of seaweeds, there are three abundant and obvious varieties that will make a good introduction. I hope that once you've developed a taste and appreciation for these foods, you'll be encouraged to study and search for others. As with most foods new to our palates, it is a good idea to sample their flavors gradually, as they may take some getting used to.

Once foraged and washed in salt water, seaweeds will keep in a cooler along with fresh land vegetables. For use throughout the year, they can be completely dried (in the sun or in a 100° to 150° oven with the door ajar) and then stored in an airtight container. Do not wash or soak them in fresh water until ready to be used. Recipes for seaweeds in the second section range from soup dishes to desserts. It might be surprising to hear that even a liquor has been made from seaweed!

Rockweeds

Fucus

The most common seaweed is rockweed or bladder wrack. It covers intertidal rocks and ledges with a brown-green, slippery surface that should be traversed with great caution by rockweed foragers. There are many look-alike species of rockweed and they are all equally usable. Their flat branched fronds — some end in small popable air bladders — are not actually eaten, although a tea can be brewed from them. Rockweed is used most frequently as a flavoring agent when cooking seafoods such as periwinkles or mussels (clams and lobsters, too) alone or in fish soups and chowders. Consult recipes for each, including rockweed tea in the second section.

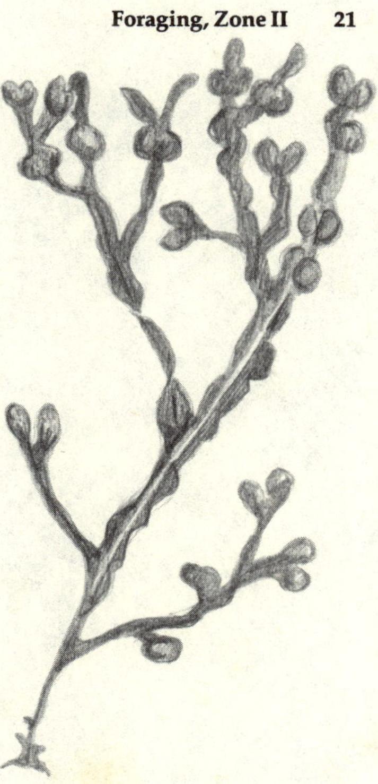

Irish Moss

Chondrus crispus

In general, the seaweed that has been making its way surreptitiously into many of the foods we eat is known as Irish moss or sea moss. Carrageenan, a carbohydrate extract of Irish moss, is useful in food and pharmaceutical industries. When it is brought to a boil in milk or other liquids, Irish moss produces a gel that is helpful in certain recipes. The flavor, cooked texture, and nutritionally rich composition of Irish moss make it a most worthy food. It is also easy to gather.

This sea vegetable is exposed at the lowest tides (moon tide is the

best), covering rocks just below the rockweed level. It has a tightly curled leaf or blade, and ranges in color from deep olive green to pink or deep purple, being 3″ to 6″ high. You will sometimes find white pieces that have been storm cast by winds and then sun-bleached along the beach at the high-tide mark. These pieces are edible (and, in fact, have a higher carrageenan content), although they are not as high in vitamins as fresh Irish moss. Never eaten raw, pliable wet Irish moss becomes very tough when dried, but a brief boiling in fresh water makes it tender again.

Because dried Irish moss stores so well, collect large bagfuls of it. Use what you like for a foraged meal and dry the rest; you can use it for months and even years to come. Dry Irish moss either on a rack in the sun or in a slow oven (100° to 150° or so) with the door ajar. Do not seal it in a storage container until all the moisture has evaporated. To reconstitute it, first crumple and shake the stiff bunches to loosen particles of sand and debris. Then swish the moss in four or five changes of fresh water. Proceed to soak and use as directed in the recipes for Irish moss.

When chopped or picked apart into small pieces, this seaweed, fresh or dried, can be added to almost all soups and stews. It will act as a thickener and make your dish more nutritious and good tasting.

Edible Kelp

Alaria esculenta

You may already be familiar with *wakame,* the Japanese relative of our edible kelp. *Wakame* has made its way into some menus via the macrobiotic route. Edible kelp can be successfully substituted for its Japanese cousin in recipes.

Also called alaria, this sea vegetable has a long, thin, olive brown, sinuous frond (ranging from 1′ to 12′ in length). Edible kelp is found attached to rocks and ledges below the low-tide level, or partially exposed only during a very low moon tide. Generally, it is good to plan to wade into the water when the tide is lowest and, using a knife, cut off the long ribbed stalk with its ruffled edges. If you cut the stalk just above the distinctive bladed fronds that fan out near the bottom of the stalk, you allow the remaining lateral flat blades to continue producing new growth. This is a bit of a sacrifice, as it is these lateral blades that are the most delicious. Sometimes, however, entire fronds are washed ashore after storms, and one can then enjoy the tasty fertile blades in good conscience. It's worth collecting large quantities. Use part fresh, and dry the rest for later use. To dry kelp, wash it in salt water first; then place it on a rack in the sun, or in an oven (at 100° to 150° or so) with the oven door ajar to allow the moisture to escape. Kelp can be used either as whole fronds or as smooth pieces that have been cut away from both sides of the midrib. Store in sealed containers or plastic bags. Before using dried alaria, it should be soaked overnight in fresh water to cover.

Consult recipes in the second section.

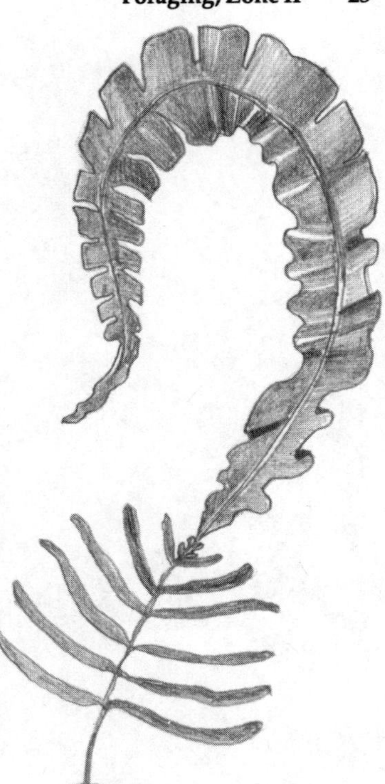

Zone III
The Shoreline — by Seasons

THE SHORELINE IS AN AREA that can be foraged at any time since it is unaffected by the tides. It is here, however, that the forager must be aware of possible trespassing. Use common sense to determine whether or not it is advisable to forage in a particular area. The section, "Resources and State Agencies," at the back of this book lists various public lands where visitors may gather and camp.

Not all public lands are open for foraging. Current State Park regulations do not allow removal of anything "natural" from the parks, so do not attempt to forage on these lands. Access to the state designated bird nesting areas is forbidden during nesting periods (generally from May 1 through July 15). During the rest of the year certain recreational uses are allowed — including "wild crop harvesting."

The state does license other uses of public lands and waters (e.g., for lumbering, oil exploration, fishing, and hunting), and it seems that granting forager's licenses would also make sense. The state would thus actually have more control over the activity. The fact remains, though, that the forager alone is responsible for his actions, and *must* avoid unnecessary trampling and over-harvesting of the foods. If you are in doubt as to whether to forage in a certain area, don't collect until you have checked with the appropriate state agency (listed at the back of this book).

The winds and tides change the shape of the shoreline daily. They have also influenced the evolution of the plants that grow there, which seem to thrive on their flirtation with the salt spray. When walking in this area, pick your path with care and avoid stepping needlessly on living plants. Since the recipes given in this book do not use the roots of the plants you will forage (with the exception of the dandelion, which is foraged whole) I suggest that you only cut off some of the stems and leaves. This allows the roots to remain in the soil and the plant will continue to grow. None of the cited plants is endangered, but it is important to keep them from becoming so. Make an attempt to pick only as many vegetables as you intend to use.

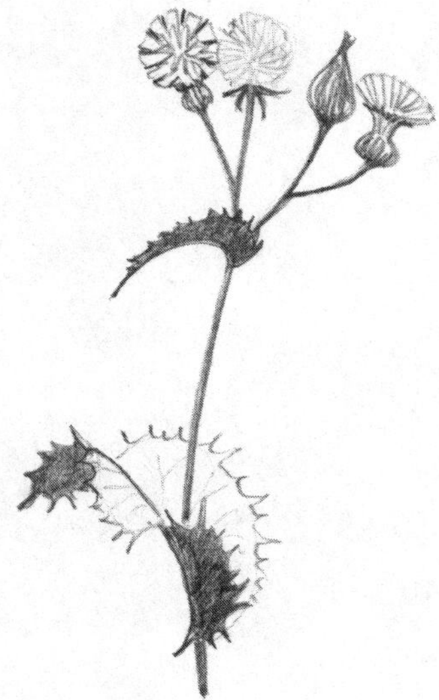

Spring and Early Summer

Greens

"Greens" is the collective name for the varied wild plants whose leaves and stems are eaten raw in the early spring, or cooked up, later in the season, as boiled potherbs. If you plan to cook these greens — one variety at a time, or in combination — you will need to collect twice what you would for a salad. Besides having excellent flavor, greens are a good source of vitamins and minerals. And they are free for the foraging and eating.

Dandelion

Taraxacum officinale

The dandelion, whose yellow blossom turns into a wish-upon round puff, is one of the world's best known flowers. It has a hollow stem that secretes a milky sap when cut. Its green leaves are long and deeply toothed. Although the whole plant can be used in many ways, it is the young spring leaves, lying directly on the ground in tight rosettes, that are eaten raw, as salad fare.

To find these plants, you'll need to get down on your knees to hunt in the grassy edge of the shoreline. The leaves are most desirable when the plants are young, before the telltale blossoms would easily lead you to them. Gather the tender young leaves into a raised bunch, exposing the root. With a sharp knife, cut around the deep, long root and remove the entire young plant, root and all. It is now easy to separate the young leaves from any surrounding grasses. Cut off the root and wash the leaves by floating them in a large amount of water.

When dry, use young dandelion leaves in fresh, raw salads. This way, no nutrients are lost through cooking. As they mature, the leaves become bitter, but are still serviceable as the most famous of potherbs: cooked dandelion greens. Unopened flower buds are also good to pan fry and eat.

Wild Lettuce

Lactuca canadensis

This is a prickly plant which can grow as high as nine feet. Like the dandelion, a thick white milk oozes out when the stalk is cut. Wild lettuce has two types of leaves along its thin stalk. The most edible are the large indented ones that look like huge dandelion leaves and are found on the lower end of the stalk; the small upper leaves are not indented. These lower leaves are long, shiny, and bright green on top, a bit whitish on their undersides. For salads, pick the leaves when the plants are no more than a foot-and-a-half tall, which is only for a brief time. For most of the season, the leaves and stems make a fantastic potherb even when too old to be eaten raw. Once the plant forms seed stalks, this green becomes too bitter to eat.

Sow Thistle

Sonchus arvensis

Sow thistle is also called beach lettuce, since it is often found along the shoreline. Its leaves are yellow green, prickly, and spiny-toothed. When mature, the stalk is three or four feet high and secretes a white sap when cut. The leaves are arranged all along the stem and bear a resemblance to those of the dandelion, its cousin. Pick the basal or lower leaves in spring or early summer; these are the newest and most tender of the leaves. Try them raw in salads, perhaps mixed with other wild greens. Sow thistle leaves are also good as boiled potherbs.

Chickweed

Stellaria media

Poultry and most birds make a beeline for this crisp and juicy green, which we use in salads or as a cooked vegetable. Chickweed begins each spring as a tight clump of stems and small (¼″) leaves. These are oval in shape with a point at the free end and are arranged along the stem in pairs. As the season progresses, the stems grow to a foot or so, branching out in radial fashion along the earth, like a groundcover. The leaves grow larger (¾″ long) but stay crisp and mild in their taste until frost.

As the plant matures, a delicate and starlike white blossom appears — the reason for its botanical name of *Stellaria*. The flower has five petals that close up at night to reopen in the sun's light.

Chickweed is the most tender and mild of all wild greens and is a particular favorite among newcomers to wild cuisine. As a cooked vegetable, it requires very little cooking, and blends well with stronger-flavored foraged foods. It is worth the effort to become familiar quickly with chickweed, for it can be eaten at any time during the summer season and grows profusely in many areas along Maine's coast. Stems and leaves of this plant can be dried and later used in stocks and soups with excellent results.

Orach
Atriplex patula

Seaside Lamb's Quarters
Chenopodium album

Both orach and lamb's quarters, members of the same family, can be used throughout the season, from early spring until autumn. When very young, the entire plant can be eaten raw or cooked, and later, the leaves alone can be used as a mild and somewhat salty potherb.

A common and abundant weed, orach can be found along the seashore, growing straight up in the air or lying limply on the rocks. The leaves are wedge shaped and can vary in length from ½″ to 3″. They are dark bluish-green in color and unevenly toothed with a bit of white, powdery covering. When you break a leaf, it will have the crispness of spinach, its botanical relative. Tasted raw, orach is a bit salty.

Seaside lamb's quarters may be located further from the shore than orach. Its upper leaves are shaped like arrowheads, while the lower leaves are more toothed and roughly diamond shaped. Lamb's quarters have spiked clusters of tiny green flowers. These turn into small green and then black seeds which can number in the thousands for each plant. These are edible when ground up and used in baking and cereals.

Curled Dock

Rumex crispus

Dock's distinctive appearance and wide distribution make it easy to gather. The plant grows from one to three feet in early summer, to five feet by autumn. The wavy-edged leaves, which are dark green, narrow, and lance shaped, grow out from a central root. These leaves can grow to be quite long, but the more edible ones range from 4″ to 12″ in length.

Pick a good quantity of this fine lemon-flavored vegetable when it's very young, to be used in salads with other tender wild greens, or cook it as a potherb, alone or in combination.

A handsome seed head forms later in the season. The seeds can be used in cooked cereals and in pancakes. Whole dock seed stalks go nicely in dried-flower arrangements.

Mustard

Brassica nigra

A prolific and durable weed, mustard grows everywhere, sometimes even claiming parts of the beach. It can grow four or five feet tall on thin stems and has a lovely yellow flower with four petals arranged in a cross pattern. The leaves at the bottom of the young plant are used raw in salads or cooked as greens. Leaves near the tops of the stems are elongated in shape and more bitter. The blossoms, which are about ½″ in diameter, can be thrown raw into salads, and taste a bit like broccoli.

Beach Peas

Lathyrus japonicus

When you come upon a profusion of beach peas it is not hard to imagine eating them — they are so like the larger garden-grown varieties. Clumps of these foot-high plants can ring a beach area with a profusion of pale green stems ending in pink and dark purple flowers. They develop pods which sport the curling corkscrew tendrils characteristic of the pea family. If you don't pick the blossoms they will go on to produce peapods. Newly formed, the pods are thin, with the discernible bulges of peas within. To eat these pods whole, pick only the youngest ones.

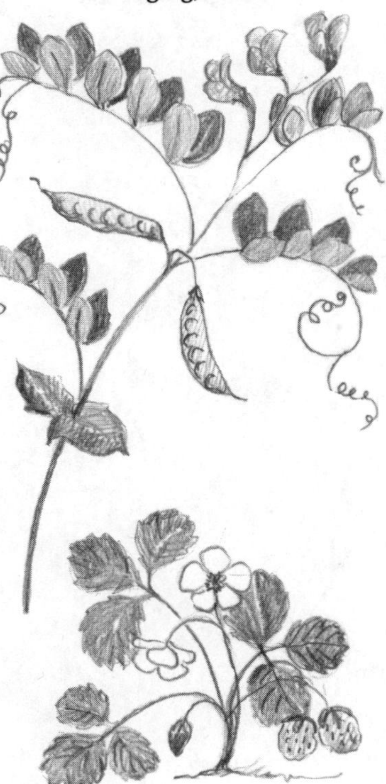

Wild Strawberries

Fragaria vesca

The first of the wondrous, edible wild berries to appear are fragrant red strawberries, which ripen in June and early July — following their beautiful white blossoms. They are easily recognized as smaller but much sweeter versions of the large domesticated berries bought in the markets. Because they are so small and low to the ground (within 6″), wild strawberries are difficult to gather in any great quantity. To pick, get right down on the grass and look for them under their larger leaves which grow in threes. Picking strawberries is a lovely way to spend a warm sunny day — you'll doubtless eat as many as you save — maybe more!

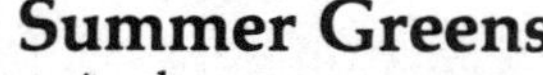

Summer Greens

As the season progresses, only the hardiest devotees of wild greens would consider eating spring greens — dandelion, wild lettuce, sow thistle, orach, seaside lamb's quarters, chickweed, wild mustard and its blossom — raw in salads. However, anyone can enjoy their mid-summer leaves, alone or in combination with other greens, as cooked potherbs. They should be brought to boil in two changes of water to soften their bitterness.

The new summer additions to greens foraged along the beach include sea rocket, goosetongue, and beach parsley. Each of these continues to put out new growth throughout the season.

Sea Rocket

Cakile edentula

This broad-branched member of the mustard family grows one to two feet in height. Its wedge-shaped leaves (about 2″ long) have wavy edges and, like the upper stem, are delectably tender when eaten. Sea rocket is fleshy to the touch; its texture is somewhat like a garden or houseplant succulent.

The sea rocket has little purple flowers that are ¼″ wide, cross-shaped, like the mustard blossoms, and edible as well. The best thing about the flowers is that they eventually give way to large seed pods (See Autumn).

The sea rocket plant — leaves, stem, blossom — makes a fine salad green. Raw, its flavor is a bit peppery; fresh sprigs used in sandwiches add a piquant and crunchy boost. Cooked, this shore vegetable is mild and reminiscent of turnip greens.

Goosetongue

Plantago oliganthus

Also called seaside plantain, this hardy plant chooses the harshest spots along the coast as its terrain. It appears, almost miraculously, amidst cracks in rocks, bluffs, and even on the beach right along the high-tide line.

The plant consists of clusters of brittle stalklike leaves that measure from 3″ to 6″ long and up to ½″ wide. They are greyish green and show a triangular cross section when broken in two. Since goosetongue sets out new growth all summer, one can pick the newest shoots throughout the season to be eaten raw or cooked. The best foraging times are June and early July when the whole plant, less the tall flower stalk, is edible.

Beach Parsley or Beach Celery

Ligusticus scothicum

The common names for this seashore plant may arouse a conflict in your taste memory bank for it is called beach celery as well as beach parsley. The appearance of the plant belies its celery classification,

although it tastes like the two combined. Another common name is Scotch Lovage.

This plant can grow tall in some areas, but along Maine's seacoast, the winds seem to keep it low, never taller than a foot. Beach parsley has a cluster of long stalks topped with celerylike bright green leaves. When the whole stalk is pulled up, it shows red coloring at the base where the stalks are larger. The shiny individual leaves consist of three smaller leaflets which are further divided into three sharply toothed sections. When you find a plant, sometimes growing amidst rocks alone, crush a leaf and enjoy the rich fragrance reminiscent of parsley. It is very pleasant to chew.

When young, beach parsley can be used raw to flavor salads. Later in the summer, add it as a seasoning when cooking other dishes. Use it in moderation — its flavor is quite strong. The recipe section includes instructions for preparing beach parsley as a vegetable.

Another edible seaside plant, seacoast angelica (*Coelopleurum lucidum*), greatly resembles beach parsley, and actually is of the same family. It grows quite a bit taller (up to 4′), has three-forked leaflets similar to beach parsley, but has a distinctive central stalk. The younger stems and stalks can be eaten raw — usually peeled — and have a celerylike flavor. After being peeled, seacoast angelica can be cooked by boiling in a little water until tender.

Beach Peas

Lathyrus japonicus

In the summer season, beach peas are delicious and special when served shelled. This late in the season, the pods will be too tough to eat whole. They are a good item to seek when you have youngsters foraging with you since they are plentiful and easy to find. Extra help and patience, however, may be necessary; a lot of pea pods must be picked and shelled to make enough for a meal.

Mints

Mentha

Peppermint (*M. piperita*) and wild mint (*M. arvensis*) are the most common mints in this area. They are easy to recognize by their squarish stems, their opposite-paired leaves, and, of course, by the familiar fragrance of their leaves when squeezed.

Both plants have long pointed leaves (1″ to 2″ long) with saw-toothed edges. In the peppermint, a pale purple cluster of blossoms forms as the plant matures, forming a tall spike at the top of each branch. But on the wild mint, small blossoms are found at the union of each leaf to the stalk (the leaf axils).

Since mint is so pungent, you need to collect only a few leaves at a time for immediate use. Foraged mint leaves also can be dried and used as a seasoning in beverages and food all year. (See the recipe section.)

Red Clover

Trifolium

The dark pink blossoms of the familiar red clover plant are of interest not only to the bees, but to the forager as well. Delicately fragrant, the full and puffy blossoms are abundant through summer, and even into autumn. They are edible right off the plant and can be chewed as you go about foraging for other plants. They are a visual and taste delight when made into a cup of freshly brewed tea, alone or in combination with other flavors. (See recipes.)

Red clover can grow as high as three feet; each plant has the familiar three-leaved — and sometimes four-leaved — configuration.

Bayberry

Myrica pensylvanica

This shrub commonly grows to about three feet in height and is often called wax myrtle. It grows along the seashore in large, distinctive clumps easily identified by its grey branches and shiny green leaves.

The narrow leaves (1½″ to 3″ long) stand erect on the end of their stiff branches and have a strong aromatic scent when they are crushed. They are evergreen and can be gathered at any time during the season and air-dried for winter use.

Berries

As summer progresses, the warmth and glow of the sun seem to be captured within ripened wild berries. When picked midday in the sun, their flavors are particularly intense. Since most people are familiar with the different kinds of berries, only brief foraging information follows.

Blueberries

Vaccinium augustifolium

Maine blueberries grow on bushes of different heights, but the 6″ to 10″ low-bush variety is most frequent near the shore. It often grows right beside great rocks and ledges and marks the transition to grassy areas.

Blueberries ripen from mid-July into August, turning to shades of red and blue as they mature. Since most people are accustomed to large, showy, cultivated blueberries, it helps to be aware that these berries are very small in comparison, ¼″ or so in diameter. They can be identified by the small, pointy-edged crown that tops them. These berries are borne by thornless plants with small, ½″ oval leaves. The ripened fruit has a few barely noticeable seeds within its soft, sweet pulp.

Raspberries and Blackberries

Rubus family

These berry delicacies are related to each other and to their store-bought cousins, making them easily recognized in the wild. Both are superb to eat even though their seeds can be annoying if they get

wedged between your teeth — but most agree that they are well worth this minor aggravation! Their colors range from the raspberry's deep pink to the glossy bluish-black of the black raspberry or blackberry.

Raspberry plants grow from one to five feet, have prickly canes and bright green three-part leaves. When picking ripe raspberries (mid-July until autumn), you will find that they easily drop off their white cone-shaped hulls, creating a cup at the center of each berry.

Blackberry canes are much more serious to deal with. They can reach 10 feet in strong, brambly length and possess true thorns capable of scarring your arms. Be forewarned and wear a long-sleeved garment when seeking these worthy fruits. An oar, long stick or board can be used to push the canes apart and make it possible to pick over a densely intertwined area.

Blackberries are a bit more elongated than raspberries. They ripen from mid-August into autumn, with the berries at the top of each cluster ripening first.

Note: Once the raspberry plant has flowered and produced fruit, be certain to pick a few leaves to use in teas. Consult recipes in the second section.

Late Summer and Autumn

Wild Apples

Pyrus malus

Wild apples can sometimes be spotted close to the shoreline in meadows or open woods. When you're foraging along the coast, if it looks like there are apple trees nearby, it is worth investigating. Apple trees turned wild can yield the most flavorful fruit, which ripens by late summer and into autumn. In general, the wild apples are small, and they may have been pecked by birds or infiltrated by worms. One can usually eat or cut around these minor imperfections. Wild apples are delicious raw or cooked and their deep flavor is worth their search.

Rose Hips

Rosa rugosa

If you spend any time along Maine's coast in the summer, it is difficult not to notice the wild rugosa roses that thrive in salt air. It is common to see these wild, vigorous plants just beyond the beach area. By late August, the showy pink roses have given way to a seed fruit called the rose hip, which can be as big as 1¼″ in diameter. When fully ripened, the rose hip looks like a small plump tomato, or even a small orange-red wild apple.

Rose hips have become known in recent years because of their high vitamin C content. You can see rose hips in the wild and eat them right off the rose bush, helping yourself to this storehouse of the acclaimed vitamin. The best time to gather these hips for edibility is right after they have turned from orange to ripe red, for the longer they remain on the stem, the hairier the seeds within become. If you are primarily interested in their vitamin potential, rose hips should be gathered after they've been nipped by a frost. Use your fingers to remove the seeds, and then eat the hips just as they are. Find recipe suggestions in the second section.

Since rose hips grow toward the tops of dense prickly clumps that can reach eight or nine feet in height, a tall forager may be an essential. Or, as with blackberry picking, you can use an oar, long stick, or board to maneuver the branches down toward you.

The hips of roses other than rugosa roses may be collected and eaten safely. They will be smaller and a bit more elongated in shape than the squat, roundish fruit of the rugosa, but they, too, are a good source of vitamin C.

Note: Do not use copper or aluminum utensils when collecting or cooking rose hips. Contact with these metals lowers vitamin C potency dramatically, and the acidity of the fruit may darken the metal and result in an unpleasant metallic taste.

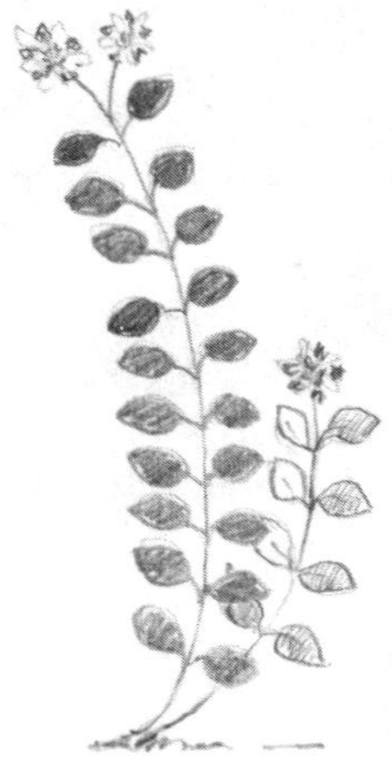

Late Summer Greens

(Lamb's quarters, chickweed, curled dock, beach parsley, sea rocket seed pods, and beach peas.)

These greens keep producing new growth until frost. Look for them in the autumn and cook them up as potherbs.

Autumn lamb's quarters can be identified by the dark seeds found at the junction of the stems and stalk. Unlike other autumn greens, lamb's quarters is always mild, and this helps to make it a rewarding plant for foraging. Remember that this plant may grow a bit inland from the actual shoreline.

Chickweed sends out new growth even after the first mild frost. The size of the leaves can vary greatly, from tiny ½″ new leaves to the matured 1½″ ones. Both stems and leaves can still be used as potherbs.

Dock is another plentiful and valuable food for the autumn forager; it sets out new leaves during warm autumn spells right up until hard frost. You can identify dock by the straight central stalk bursting with seeds, which are well in evidence in early autumn, unless they have been blown away or picked!

Beach parsley is a hardy little plant available well into fall. Its raw flavor may be too strong for all but the most dedicated foragers, but cooked it still is capable of noble duty as a flavoring or stewed vegetable.

Sea rocket's fleshy green seedpods appear on the plant by August. The pods measure approximately 1″ in length and have two distinct sections: the top part is pointed while the bottom is globular. They can be chewed raw and resemble raw cauliflower with a bite something like horseradish. When cooked, alone or with other greens, the pods of the sea rocket plant become milder in taste and are awfully good. The younger leaves can also be collected now and served in cooked fare.

By late summer, beach peas have passed their delicate prime and it's best to use them as you would store-bought dried peas. Cook them; squeeze or strain to separate the pulp from the coarse hulls. They can be collected well into the autumn when the peas are dried, yellow to brown, and hard within their pods. They will soften in cooking.

Refer to the second section for further recipe instructions.

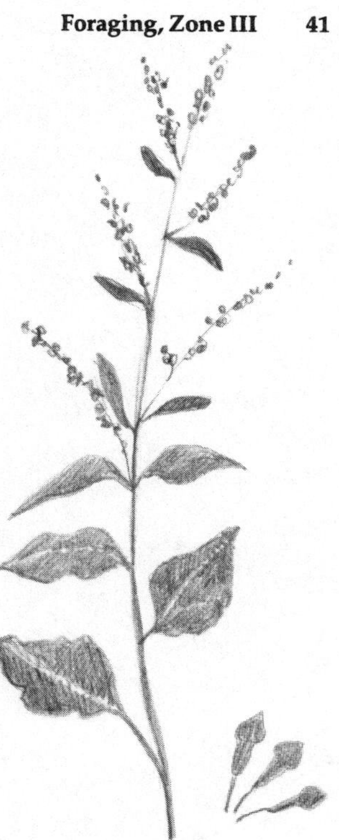

Section II — Recipes

Introduction to the Recipes

SINCE THIS BOOK is addressed to people on vacations, these recipes call for simple kitchen or galley equipment — and seldom require an oven. They can, of course, be adapted for a more complete kitchen.

Capers, pimentos, and other more exotic ingredients have not been included in the recipes but certainly can be added according to individual taste and availability. Any unusual ingredients, e.g., saffron or fresh ginger, are optional, though they are characteristic in the recipes in which they are called for.

Salt and pepper are always optional and salt should be used with discretion when cooking with sea water.

Except where noted, the recipes with specified amounts of ingredients make four servings.

Finally, one should expect stronger tastes when serving wild foods. Think in terms of slow trials and small portions to encourage acceptance of these new and wonderful foods.

Zone I
Sea Water

Fried Pollack or Cunner

fillets, or whole cleaned fish
flour, fine cracker or bread crumbs, or cornmeal with oregano,
salt and pepper, and parsley to taste,
beaten egg, with milk or water
a few tablespoons of oil

Mix the seasonings with the flour, crumbs, or cornmeal. Dip the fish in the egg mixture, then press into dry ingredients, coating each side with the seasoning mixture. Prepare a frying pan with a thin layer of oil and heat it just to smoking stage. Lower the heat a bit, add the fish, and cook about 10 minutes. Carefully turn the fish over and cook the other side, raising the heat a bit as you start the new side. After a minute or so, lower the heat again. You might choose to add a bit more oil to the pan. Cook until the fish flakes easily when gently pried with a fork. Don't overcook. This dish is wonderful served with a sprinkling of fresh lemon juice.

Baked Pollack or Cunner — in Wine, Milk, or Tomato Juice

fillets, or whole cleaned fish
dry white wine, milk (whole or reconstituted powdered milk)
or tomato juice
tarragon leaves, fresh or dried
salt and pepper
tomatoes (optional)
aluminum foil

Place fish, one layer deep, in a baking pan or upon a piece of foil cut large enough to allow the fish to be sealed in a packet whose edges will be tightly crimped. Sprinkle the fish with tarragon, salt, and pepper. Add just enough of the desired liquid to barely cover the fish. If a tomato is available, fresh or canned, it can be sliced and placed on top of the fish before adding the herbs. Bake for 20 to 25 minutes in an oven or place 3″ or 4″ over coals. Check to see if it is done by using a fork and lifting a flake out gently. If the fish flakes easily, remove from the heat at once, and serve.

Steamed Pollack or Cunner

fillets, or whole cleaned fish
sprigs of one of the following: fresh parsley, dill, or tarragon
(If no fresh herbs are available, dried herbs can be placed on top of the fish.)
onion slices
celery or beach parsley (Zone III); include the leaves
rockweed (Zone II)
salt and pepper
dry white wine (optional)
water

Put steamer basket or rack inside a large, covered saucepan. If using fresh herb sprigs, put them with the rockweed, celery, or beach parsley and onion slices on the rack first and then top with a single layer of fish. Add half water and half wine (or only water) to barely reach the basket or rack. Salt and pepper lightly. Cover the pot and bring to a boil; then lower the heat to maintain a simmering steam. Cook 5 to 10 minutes, depending on the thickness of the pieces of fish. This dish is elegant topped with Irish moss sauce (refer to the Zone II recipes) or a melted butter sauce.

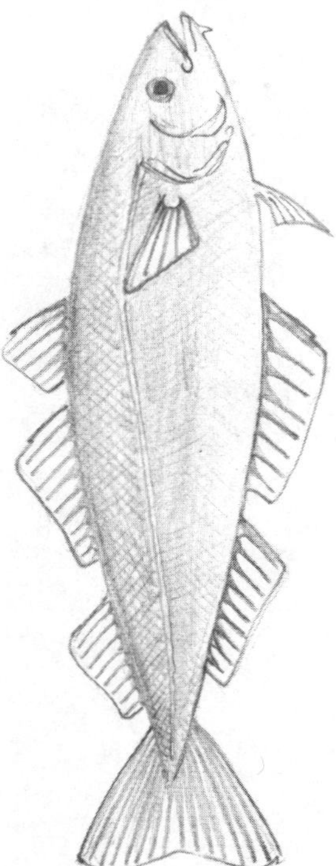

Leftover Cooked Pollack or Cunner

If you have leftover cooked fish, be certain to save it. Using your fingers, carefully remove any bones from the cooked pieces and store the leftovers in the cooler. They can be used in one of the following recipes within a day or two.

Fish Salad

leftover cooked fish, boned
mayonnaise
onions, finely chopped
herbs: tarragon, thyme, dill weed, basil or grated fresh ginger — to taste

Make a good and simple salad by mixing the leftover fish with a bit of mayonnaise, onion to taste, and a pinch of one or two of the herbs. Serve with cut-up tomatoes, hard-cooked eggs, cucumber, etc., on whole grain crackers or in sandwiches.

Fish Cakes

cooked fish, boned
boiled potatoes (use the same amount of potatoes as fish)
onion, finely minced
chopped fresh or dried parsley or beach parsley (Zone III)
1 egg
Tabasco or other hot sauce (optional)
allspice

nutmeg
pepper
freshly grated ginger (optional)
flour, bread, cracker crumbs, or sesame seeds
vegetable oil

Combine the cut-up cooked potatoes with the fish. Add a good measure of finely minced onion, the chopped parsley, and a few dashes of hot sauce. Sprinkle in a bit of allspice, some nutmeg, and fresh pepper. If you have fresh ginger, this gives a special touch. Stir in the egg. The mixture should be pliably moist; if it is not, add another egg.

Place a skillet or frying pan on the heat and add enough vegetable oil to liberally coat the bottom. When oil sizzles, take a handful of fish cake mixture — gauging the size of each cake by the number of portions required — and press the tops and bottoms of each fish cake into either flour, bread or cracker crumbs, or sesame seeds (these add the most flavor). Place each portion into the hot, oiled pan. Brown 5 to 8 minutes on one side, allowing a crispy crust to form. Carefully turn over each fish cake and repeat the crust making procedure. Continue in this manner until all the cakes are done, adding more oil to the pan with each new batch.

Unlike other fish dishes, fish cakes cannot be overcooked, but watch for too high heat and possible burning. Serve with lemon juice, tartar or seafood sauce, or ketchup. Plain fish cakes are very tasty as well.

Mackerel

Always try to catch more mackerel than you think you will use in one meal because: (1) you doubtless will eat more than you imagined you would, and (2) leftover mackerel is superb in the salad recipe that follows.

Although mackerel can be cooked in the same manner as pollack and cunner, there are two other ways that are especially suited to this flavorful fish. The first is a marinate-and-grill recipe, and the second calls for poaching the fish. Further recipes are for fried and baked mackerel.

Marinated and Grilled Mackerel

mackerel, filleted and cleaned as instructed in the first section. Do not skin the fish.
vegetable oil (not olive)
soy sauce
lemon juice
seasoned pepper (optional)

Make a marinade by combining equal parts of the three liquids. Usually, ¼ cup of each (a total of ¾ cup liquid) is sufficient for as many as 8 to 10 fish. Place the fillets in a shallow pan or bowl and cover with the marinade. The fish can be left to marinate awhile, but a few minutes is usually sufficient to add flavor.

Prepare a charcoal fire in a hibachi or grill, or build a wood fire in a fireplace. Allow it to burn down to glowing embers. Remove the fish from the marinade and place on a rack, skin side down, 2″ above the coals. Baste the fish often with the leftover marinade. After about 10 minutes, carefully turn the fish over and continue the process of grilling and basting. Serve, and expect to be delighted by the succulent texture and flavor of this mackerel — reminiscent of grilled beef! If there are any leftover pieces after the meal, they are delicious served cold, with or without mayonnaise.

Poached Mackerel (two versions)

mackerel, filleted and cleaned
milk, whole or reconstituted powdered milk
tarragon, fresh or dried (use more if fresh)

or,

mackerel
tomato juice
basil
oregano

Place a single layer of fillets in a shallow, wide pan (a frying pan is good), skin side up. Pour in the liquid (milk or juice) until it just covers the fish. Lay the herbs on top of the fillets. Place the pan on the heat and cook until the liquid begins to move (not a full boil) and simmer until the fish is done — 15 minutes or so. Remove the fish and serve as is, or garnished with more of the herb, chopped and sprinkled on top.

Baked Mackerel

mackerel, filleted
milk, whole or reconstituted powdered milk
tarragon, fresh or dried

Place fish in a baking pan; surround with milk and lightly sprinkle with tarragon. Bake uncovered in a 350° oven for 30 minutes.

Fried Mackerel

Almost any fish can be pan fried, but as mackerel is a bit oily, frying is the least desirable way to prepare it. Of course, lemon juice sprinkled on the fried fish helps cut the oiliness. Drain cooked mackerel briefly on paper (clean brown paper shopping bags work well).

Leftover Cooked Mackerel

Mackerel Salad

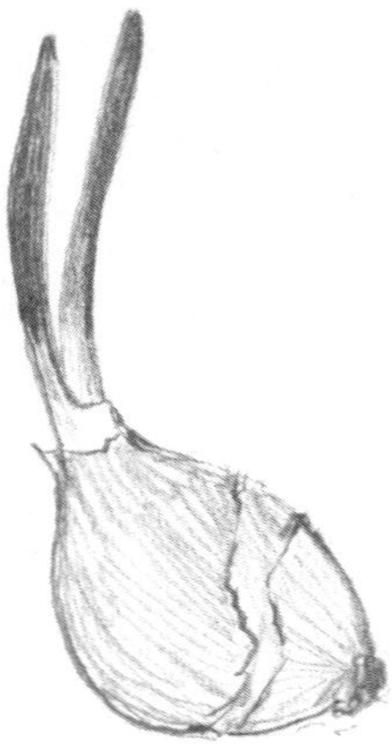

mackerel, cooked and boned
vinegar or lemon juice
celery, chopped
onion, chopped
thyme leaves
mayonnaise
sour cream (optional)
leftover cooked rice (optional)
black pepper, coarsely milled (optional)

Pick through leftover mackerel, removing any bones, fins and skin. Marinate the fish in some vinegar or lemon juice, and place in a cooler until the next day or so. For a salad, add a generous amount of chopped onion and celery, a fairly liberal dousing of thyme, a portion of cooked rice (not more than 1/3 the amount of fish), and bind all together with some mayonnaise. This can be thinned with some sour cream, if available. Since mackerel is an oily fish, go easy on the dressing. Taste and add more lemon juice or vinegar if needed. (If the mixture seems a bit too thin, use grated lemon peel rather than lemon juice.) Add some coarsely milled black pepper and taste again. Add salt if it's a bit flat.

This salad is good with greens, tomatoes, hard-boiled eggs, etc., and is delicious when eaten as a spread in sandwiches or on crackers.

Fish Soups and Chowders

In any discussion of fresh fish recipes, soups should be a major consideration, particularly when you are catching the fish and then cleaning (and filleting) them. This is because some of the parts that are generally discarded in this process are used as the major ingredients in the preparation of fish soup stock. Basic directions follow for this clear broth, which is the basis for various soups, or as cooking liquid for rice. Of course, fish can be caught with a scrumptious soup or chowder in mind. Add the boned fish as the last step in the soup's process.

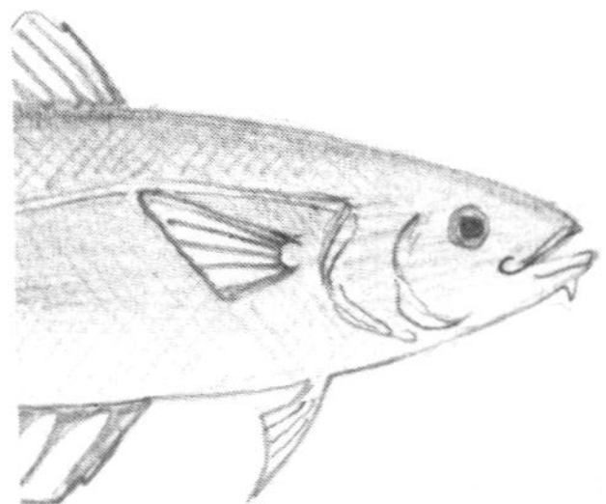

Basic Fish Stock (Court Bouillon)

fish parts (heads, bones, and scraps)
water
large onion, peeled and sliced
bayberry leaf (Zone III)
celery (optional)
carrots, 1 or 2 sliced
beach parsley (Zone III)
whole black pepper corns, or coarsely ground pepper
1 cup or so of rockweed (Zone II), optional but good for flavor
thyme, fresh or dried

When cleaning and filleting your fish, discard the intestines and all matter found in the belly cavity. Keep the head, backbone, and all other parts not used in a desired recipe. Place these leftover parts in a kettle or pot that has a top, and cover with water. Add the sliced onion, bayberry leaf, any celery leaves or stalks (a good way to use celery discards), the carrots, a few sprigs of beach parsley, and one or two whole black pepper corns or a grinding of pepper. Now add a good handful of fresh rockweed. Cover the pot, and bring to a boil. Lower the flame to maintain a simmer. Let this cook for an hour or more. When ready, take the stock off the stove, cool a bit, and then strain the liquid. It is now ready to be used in soup or chowder recipes.

Stock can be refrigerated in a covered glass jar or bowl for several days. If, after a few days, you're not ready to use it, bring the stock to a boil, cook it for five minutes, then return it to the refrigerator. It will keep safely for two or three more days. (Sniff the stock before using. "Bad" or spoiled fish products are easily detected. Be certain to discard the fish parts or stock if you have any doubts — and start afresh).

The following recipes actually improve if you keep them refrigerated for a day or two. If possible, make the dish a day ahead or plan enough for a leftover meal to be served a few days later.

Mediterranean-style Sopa de Pescado

fish broth (see preceding recipe) 1 quart more or less
2 or 3 tablespoons olive oil
2 onions, sliced
2 or 3 cloves garlic, minced
3 or 4 tomatoes, fresh or canned, with juice
3 or 4 stalks celery, chopped
½ cup green pepper, coarsely chopped
¼ teaspoon black pepper
2 or 3 threads of saffron (optional and very expensive, but adds a special and characteristic flavor)
white wine, to taste (optional)
Tabasco sauce (optional)
cooked rice or potato slices (leftovers)
fish, fresh or picked over from previously cooked fish
4 tablespoons chopped beach parsley (Zone III)

Heat the oil in a large pot or kettle and lightly sauté the sliced onions and garlic until they are soft and a bit yellow. Remove pot from the heat and allow to cool down a bit. Add the fish broth, adjusting for the amount required by adding more water or the liquid from canned tomatoes (if used). Bring to a boil. Add the tomatoes, mashing them up a bit with a spoon, the other vegetables, the black pepper and saffron (if available), and cook gently until the vegetables are tender. If desired, add some white wine, being mindful not to dilute the flavors too much. Taste for seasonings, adding a few drops of Tabasco as desired. Just before serving, add the cooked rice or the potatoes, and the fish. If you are using leftover cooked fish, it only needs to be heated through. Fresh raw fish should be added to the hot broth and vegetables and gently simmered until it flakes. Dish up the soup and sprinkle with chopped beach parsley. Serve with crackers or crusty French or Italian bread, if available. Depending on the amounts of fish, rice, or potatoes, this hardy and flavorful soup can be a filling main dish.

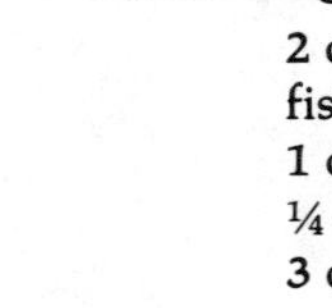

New England Fish Chowder

2 cups fish broth (see page 54)
fish fillets, or lots of picked over cooked fish
1 or 2 onions, chopped
¼ cup butter, margarine, oil, or salt pork (a half-pound piece)
3 or 4 potatoes, sliced
1 teaspoon basil
¼ teaspoon black pepper (optional)
1 can of whole kernel corn (optional)
1 tall can evaporated milk
4 tablespoons beach parsley, finely chopped

For a true downeast flavor, cut the salt pork into ¼″ cubes and fry in a skillet until the morsels are crisp and golden brown. Watch closely as they can burn easily. With a spatula or turner, lift out pieces of pork and drain them on a paper bag or paper towel. Drain ¼ cup of the liquid fat remaining in the skillet into a soup pot. If salt pork isn't convenient or doesn't appeal to you, use butter, margarine, or oil. Heat and then sauté one or two onions until limp. Cool a bit and then add two cups of strained fish broth or water and the potatoes with their skins on or off, as desired. Also add the basil and black pepper and boil until the potatoes just begin to test done — about 15 minutes. Now add one can of drained corn kernels (optional, but awfully good and filling) and bring just to the boiling point. Add the fish pieces and simmer very gently for another 10 minutes. Just before serving, add the evaporated milk and heat — watching closely so as not to allow it to boil, which might curdle the chowder.

The chowder can be kept in your refrigerator or cooler. This will heighten and blend the flavors. Always remember that when heating up the chowder, do it ever so slowly and do not allow it to boil. Traditionally, some of the fried pork scraps are sprinkled on top of each bowlful. Chopped beach parsley is a lovely addition, too.

Fish Stew

2 or 3 tablespoons olive oil, butter, margarine, or vegetable oil
2 onions, coarsely chopped
2 or 3 cloves fresh garlic, minced
1 green pepper, chopped
3 or 4 stalks celery, chopped
2 cups fish broth, water, or liquid from drained tomatoes
1 cup, approximately, of wild greens (Zone III)
½ cup Irish moss, fresh (Zone II) (optional)
1 teaspoon oregano
1 teaspoon basil
fresh fish fillets or steaks, or boned chunks of leftover cooked fish
cooked rice, potatoes, beans, or vegetables (leftovers or canned)
Tabasco (optional)
salt and pepper to taste
croutons from leftover bread (optional)

In a big pot or soup kettle, place olive oil (or butter, margarine, etc.) and gently sauté the onion slices, minced garlic, green pepper, and celery. When softened, add the liquid of your choice. Shred the greens and Irish moss and add to the pot. Now sprinkle in the desired seasonings and bring to a boil. Simmer for 20 minutes. Add the substance of the stew: the fish, rice or potatoes, the beans and/or vegetables. The exact amounts are not important; add what is available using your taste preference as a guide. This is a delicious way to clean out the refrigerator or cooler. A can of beans (limas being the usual in a fish stew) is a particularly good addition, if you have none as leftovers. Heat gently to meld the flavors and check for seasonings, adding Tabasco, more garlic, and possibly salt and pepper. Chopped beach parsley is a great garnish to add to each serving; croutons are lovely, too. This stew is elegant served with wholewheat crackers or breadsticks. As with stews in general, a fish stew is improved if it's stored a day or two before serving.

Mexican-style Fish Stew

1 cup olive oil
2 or 3 onions, chopped
1 can tomatoes (with juice) or 3 or 4 fresh tomatoes, peeled
2 cloves garlic, minced
3 stems and leaves of beach parsley, chopped (Zone III)
2 cups (approximately) pollack, cunner, or mackerel pieces, alone or in combination
6 stuffed olives (optional)
salt and pepper

In a pot, heat the oil and add the vegetables. Stew them gently while stirring. Add the pieces of fish and continue to cook over a low heat until the fish tests done. Check for salt and pepper; add olives, and serve.

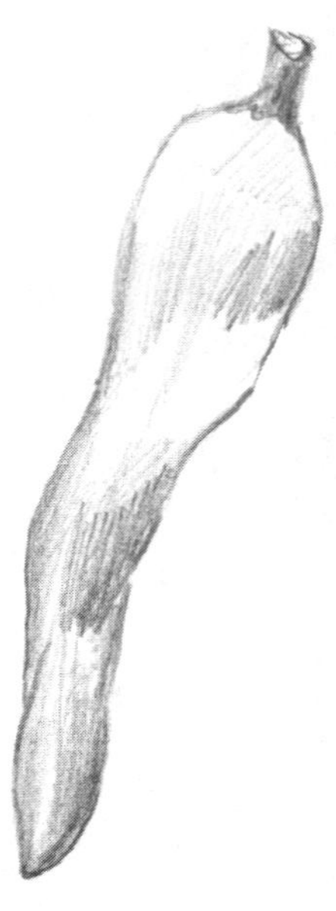

Seviche

This is the last of the fish recipes, and may be the best suited to a foraging vacation and a simplified kitchen or galley. No cooking with heat is required and no refrigeration is needed for this marvelous Latin-American dish. In addition, strips or rough squares of fish are used — often easier to prepare than neatly formed fillets. The recipe calls for one pound of fresh fish (about two cups). If desired, the recipe can be halved. Getting fresh limes and hot chili peppers to a vacation spot or aboard a boat may be a bit awkward, but since the recipe is so perfect for these situations in other ways, the effort seems warranted.

1 pound mackerel or any white fish cut into boneless strips or squares, from ¼" to ½" thick
1 cup fresh lime juice (about 6 limes) or ½ cup lime and ½ cup lemon juice
1 onion, chopped
1 garlic clove, minced
3 green chili peppers (jalapeño), seeded and chopped fine (These are generally found with Mexican food supplies.)
¼ teaspoon oregano
½ teaspoon salt
black pepper, freshly ground (optional)
¼ cup olive oil
1 fresh tomato, sliced, or cherry tomatoes (optional)
1 ripe avocado, sliced (optional)

Place fish strips or squares in a deep glass dish, or a bowl or pot made of stainless steel or enamelware. Add the freshly squeezed lime juice (or the lime and lemon juice mixture), the chopped onion, minced garlic, and the seeded, chopped green chili peppers. Also add ½ teaspoon of salt, some freshly ground black pepper, the oregano, and olive oil. Stir the mixture well and let it stand in a cool place, turning gently every three to four hours. The seviche will be "cooked" by the citric acid of the juices within three hours, but the texture and flavor improve with more time; 24 hours is a normal waiting time. If refrigeration is available, seviche can be kept and eaten for about one week. Serve garnished with tomato and avocado slices, if desired.

Crabmeat

Crabmeat has to be one of life's culinary joys. It has its own special flavor and adapts well to different kinds of dishes. It can be used in almost every stage of a meal, barring the traditional dessert slot. Who knows, some zany gourmand probably *has* made a crabmeat dessert!

If you have the time, pick out the crabmeat the day before you plan to use it and store it in a good cooler or refrigerator. A good flavor trick is to sprinkle fresh lemon juice over the meat and mix it in, before refrigerating overnight. The crabmeat can then be used in a salad or spread. If you plan to use the crabmeat creamed or in a chowder, omit the lemon juice. It would still be wise, however, to pick the meat out a day ahead; it takes a good while for the inexperienced to obtain a good quantity of clear meat. See the first section for instructions on cleaning crabs.

Pure-and-Simple Crab

crabmeat, cooked and picked out
fresh lemon quarters, or juice
crackers

Round up a bit of crabmeat upon a cracker and serve sprinkled with lemon juice. An immediate delight.

Crabmeat Spread

crabmeat, cooked and picked out
fresh lemon juice
finely chopped parsley or beach parsley (Zone III)
tarragon
finely minced onions
Tabasco (optional)
mayonnaise (optional)
crackers, or thin slices of cucumber

Combine crabmeat and lemon juice, tossing lightly with chopped parsley, tarragon, and finely minced onion. Add a squirt of Tabasco if wished. This can all be bound with mayonnaise, but it is not necessary. It is lighter, and less fattening if mixed with lemon juice only. Provide crackers, bread, and cucumber slices for the spread. Crackers will become soggy if prepared in advance.

Crabmeat Salad

This is one of those dishes that can be made as elaborately as one wishes, but the simplest concoctions may well be the best.

crabmeat, cooked and picked out
lemon juice, preferably fresh
thyme
black pepper, freshly ground (optional)
onion, finely minced
mayonnaise, evaporated milk, or cream
chili sauce (optional)

Drizzle a bit of lemon juice on your crabmeat. Add some thyme, black pepper, and minced onion to taste. Bind all together with a spoonful or two of mayonnaise thinned with some evaporated milk or cream, if wished. Serve on a bed of lettuce, or in fresh tomatoes that have been cut open in rosette form. Crabmeat salad is spectacular when served in a ripened avocado half. A dash of chili sauce is lovely, but not necessary, as a final topping.

Other food items that combine well with crabmeat are: drained canned pineapple chunks, chopped hard-boiled eggs, and sweet pickle relish.

Crabmeat Bisque (a milk soup)

If you plan to make a crab bisque or soup, remember to save some of the steaming liquid from the cooking pot, once you drain the crabs. This becomes the stock or base of the finished soup. Real devotees even take the bodies (shells) and break them up to be boiled in the stock. The resulting strained liquid is quite rich and flavorful; lovely, but not essential to a good crab soup or bisque.

crab stock, 2 cups or so (use water if stock is not available)
one cupful of crabmeat, cooked and picked out
3 tablespoons flour
4 tablespoons butter, margarine, or oil
dry sherry (optional, but distinctive and good in a bisque)
1 cup evaporated milk
thyme
nutmeg
bayberry leaf (Zone III)
paprika
leftover cooked rice (optional)

First, make a cream sauce by melting the butter in a large soup pot. Add the flour and stir until blended into a smooth paste. Slowly pour in about two cups of the crab stock or water, and stir all the while to prevent lumps from forming. Now add one cup of evaporated milk and continue stirring until just heated through. Add the thyme to taste, the bayberry leaf, and a dash of nutmeg. Then add the rice (if used) and the crabmeat — a cup of crabmeat, at least, to these proportions, but you cannot go wrong by adding more. The amount of liquid can be adjusted to the right thickness. When thoroughly heated through, add a splash of sherry. (Note: scotch whiskey is called for in some recipes in lieu of sherry. Use whatever tastes best to you.) Ladle into individual bowls and sprinkle with paprika. As with most milk-based soups, the flavor is greatly enhanced if the bisque is made a day or two ahead and kept cold in a refrigerator. Do not attempt to keep a seafood and milk soup without good refrigeration.

Creamed Crab

Here is a basic recipe for creamed crab which can be fiddled with as conditions and your larder allow. Some possible variations are: cheese in the sauce, a bit of curry for seasoning, some steamed young beach peas, lightly sautéed mushroom pieces, toasted almonds, chopped hard-boiled eggs, or egg yolks added to the sauce (which will make the end result a good deal richer).

crabmeat, cooked and picked out (1 cup or more)
2 or 3 tablespoons butter, margarine, or oil
2 or 3 tablespoons flour
½ teaspoon tarragon (optional)
½ teaspoon dry mustard
½ cup white wine or water
½ cup evaporated milk
chopped beach parsley for edible garnish (Zone III)
paprika

Make a basic cream sauce (see recipe for crabmeat bisque) with the flour, butter (margarine or oil), white wine, and evaporated milk. Adjust proportions of butter, flour, wine or water for the right consistency; some prefer a thicker sauce than others. If water is substituted for wine, use the crab cooking water. Add the tarragon and dry mustard, if wished, and then at least a cup of crabmeat, more if possible. Heat through, stirring gently, and serve on cooked rice with chopped beach parsley, sprinkle each serving with a bit of paprika. Some young beach peas (Zone III), simmered in milk, are a good accompaniment to this memorable dish.

Crab Cakes

2 tablespoons butter, margarine, or oil
1 small onion, finely chopped
½ cup cracker or bread crumbs
1 cup crabmeat, cooked and picked out
1 egg, beaten
½ teaspoon salt
½ teaspoon dry mustard
2 tablespoons parsley, beach or regular, finely chopped
evaporated milk
flour or more fine bread crumbs

Heat the butter in a skillet and gently sauté the chopped onion until soft; add the crumbs to the skillet. Mix the onion-and-crumb mixture in a bowl with the crabmeat, beaten egg, and seasonings. Stir well, adding enough evaporated milk to hold the ingredients together when shaped into four fairly large flat cakes. Dip both sides of each cake into the flour, and brown in butter or oil in a heated skillet. Brown the cakes on each side and cook through. Serve with seafood or tartar sauce, or lemon juice.

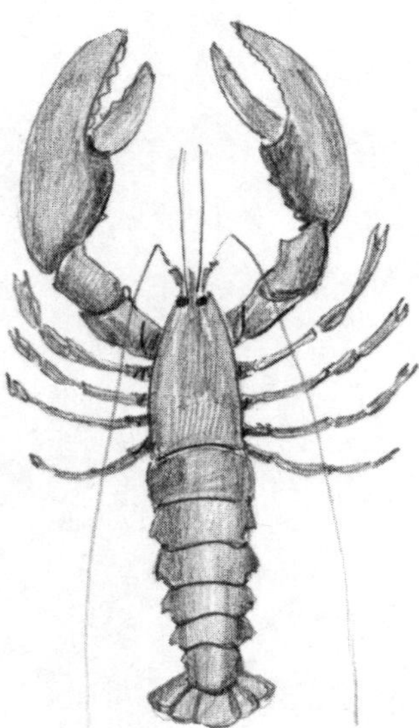

Lobster

Once purchased, lobsters only require cooking — no cleaning is necessary. Lobsters can be a prime ingredient in a regal shoreline clambake (see p. 79) but they are more often served steamed (or boiled) in Maine. Steaming lobsters is preferable as less water will accumulate in the shells, and the succulent flavor seems to be more intense.

To steam lobsters, add the lobsters to one or two inches of fiercely boiling sea water, or water with some salt added, in a large, covered pot. Pick up the lobsters by their large backs and thrust one live lobster at a time into the water headfirst to quick-kill. When all are in, cover the pot, maintain a high heat, and bring to a boil again as quickly as possible. Do not be surprised when there is involuntary reflex action in the dead lobsters. In 15 minutes from when the steam reappears the lobsters should have turned the characteristic red-orange. If some still have decidedly dark areas of black or dark green, steam another five minutes, but no longer. Eat them fresh and hot, with hot drawn butter ready, some lemon, and maybe vinegar. Indescribably good.

Recipes for Leftover Cooked Lobster

Note: The proportion of lobster to other ingredients in the recipes can vary, depending on how much meat is available, the number of guests, and the proportion of lobster required.

Simplified Lobster Newburg (without egg yolks)

1 to 2 cups cooked, picked-out lobster meat
¼ to ½ cup sherry
1½ cups of a rich cream sauce (2 tablespoons flour, ¼ cup butter, 1½ cups milk)
½ cup cream, or evaporated milk
pinch of paprika
½ teaspoon curry powder (optional)

Soak lobster meat in sherry, turning occasionally. This can be done overnight, or in a half-hour if pressed for time. Make the cream sauce (see p. 64), stir in lobster and sherry, paprika, and curry powder. Heat gently, stirring constantly. When heated through, add the cream and heat again. This is usually served over rice.

Lobster Stew

Note: This should be made at least 5 hours ahead of serving time for optimum traditional flavor.

cooked meat, tomalley (liver), and coral (roe) from one small lobster per person, cut up in small pieces
2 tablespoons of butter per lobster
1 teaspoon finely chopped onion (optional) per lobster
1 cup milk per lobster
salt and pepper

Melt butter in saucepan (or double boiler) and simmer the tomalley and coral a few minutes; then add the cut-up lobster meat and heat through. Add the chopped onion, if used. Pour in milk; stir to blend, and heat but don't boil. Taste for salt and pepper. Now, let this all rest for 5 hours uncovered, until it reaches room temperature. Then cover and refrigerate. Do not allow to boil when reheated. Serve piping hot. Pilot crackers go well with this stew.

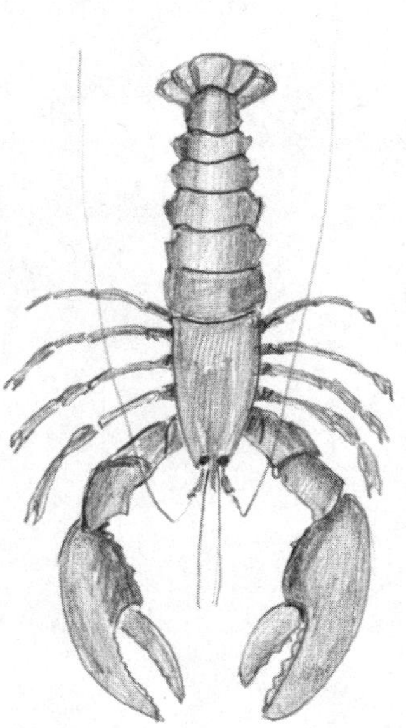

Quick Zesty Lobster

½ cup (1 stick) melted butter, or margarine
2/3 cup chili sauce
2 tablespoons finely chopped onion
1 tablespoon finely chopped beach parsley (Zone III)
2 tablespoons lemon juice
salt
2 to 4 cups cooked, diced lobster meat
hot sauce (optional)

Combine all ingredients except the lobster meat and hot sauce in a saucepan. Simmer for a few minutes and then add the meat and hot sauce (if wished). Taste for flavor, and stir while heating gently. Serve right away on cooked rice, cous-cous, or pasta.

Lobster Bisque and Lobster Salad

For these recipes, consult crabmeat recipes (pages 63 and 64), as the directions and ingredients are basically the same. The ingredients can be augmented with leftover cooked fish, too.

Scallops

As purchased, scallops are ready to use in recipes, with no wasted weight of shells, etc. As a guide, one pound is sufficient for three servings. Perhaps broiled scallops (5 to 6 minutes) are the most popular, but recipes that do not require use of an oven will be suggested here. (Note: Fresh scallops can also be eaten raw, in the manner of oysters.)

Grilled Scallops

1½ to 2 pounds scallops
1/3 cup each: oil, lemon juice, and soy sauce
¼ teaspoon black pepper

Make a marinade from the ingredients listed above; let the scallops marinate for a few hours in the mixture. Then thread them loosely on a skewer (perhaps interspersed with green pepper sections, parboiled whole onions, tomato quarters). Cook over prepared coals on a hibachi, or campfire, basting with leftover marinade, and turning until the scallops are white and firm throughout — about 5 to 7 minutes. Serve with lemon quarters and additional soy sauce.

Savory Scallop Sauté

1½ to 2 pounds of scallops
flour for dredging
½ cup butter or olive oil
3 cloves of garlic, pressed or finely minced
salt and pepper to taste
½ cup chopped beach parsley (Zone III) or regular parsley
1 teaspoon crushed or chopped tarragon

Wash scallops and drain, then roll them about in the flour to coat well. Heat the butter or oil until quite hot; add the scallops and garlic and toss quickly and evenly. Cook from 5 to 7 minutes until the meat is firm and white throughout. Sprinkle with salt and pepper and remove from the fire. Immediately add parsley and tarragon, and stir until evenly distributed. A dash of lemon or vinegar is good, too. Delicious!

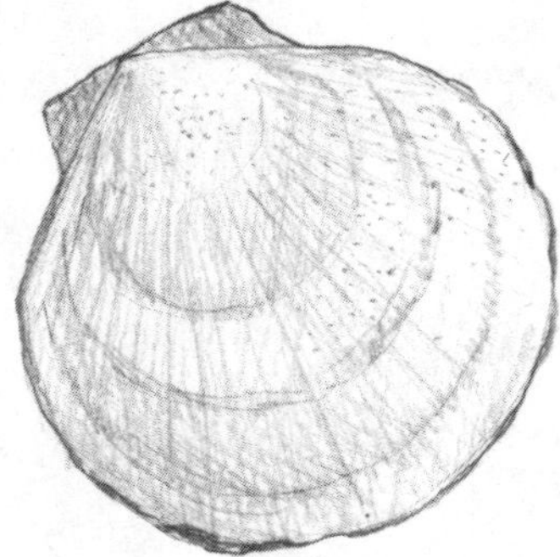

Poached Scallops

white (dry) cooking wine
1 or 2 onions, sliced
1 bayberry leaf (Zone III)
freshly ground black pepper (optional)
scallops

Gently heat white wine in a wide skillet until simmering. Add onion slices and then distribute the scallops evenly over the pan bottom. Top with a grinding of black pepper, if wished. Cover and simmer ever so gently until the scallops are cooked through and are white — 5 to 7 minutes.

Cold Scallop Salad and Scallop Stew

Scallops can be used in many of the same recipes as crabmeat (see pages 62–66).

For scallop stew, 1½ cups of scallops are added to one quart of milk. Use 2 tablespoons butter when making the cream sauce. Worcestershire sauce or curry powder are lovely additions.

Zone II
Intertidal Land

Mussels

Steamed Mussels

Allow two dozen mussels per person, and even more if this is to be the main dish. If there are leftovers, use them in the spaghetti-sauce recipes (page 75).

mussels
a handful of rockweed (Zone II)
several sprigs of beach parsley (Zone III)
1 or 2 onions, sliced
2 or 3 cloves garlic, slivered (Use more if you're a garlic lover.)
2 bayberry leaves (Zone III)
1 cup white wine or water
¼ teaspoon black pepper (optional)

Once scrubbed and de-bearded (as described on page 17), the easiest and perhaps the most delicious way to prepare mussels is to place them in a large skillet or steamer kettle that can be covered with a lid or a piece of foil. Add the wine or water (or a combination of the two), the onion slices, garlic, bayberry leaves, beach parsley, and the handful of fresh rockweed. Cover and bring to a rapid boil; lower the heat and gently simmer. Cook for 15 minutes or until the mussels have opened wide. As with any bivalve, only eat those that have opened; discard the others. Serve the mussels in a bowl with some of the broth, which is wonderfully tasty all by itself. The steamed mussels can be eaten plain or with drawn butter. Crusty French bread is a traditional accompaniment but if you have any leftover or newly cooked rice, it's delicious added to the hot broth. To eat, pick the meat out of each shell. May you find this a superb taste treat.

Note: Be certain to save some of the broth if planning to make a sauce for any leftovers (see following recipe).

Stewed Mussels

steamed mussels (see preceding recipe)
3 tablespoons butter, margarine, or oil
3 tablespoons flour
1½ cups broth from the steamed mussels, or a combination of broth and/or water and milk
salt and pepper to taste

After following the directions for steamed mussels, remove one shell and the remaining beard from each mussel and place on a serving dish. Keep them warm while you prepare the following sauce. Melt the butter over heat and make a cream sauce by adding the flour, and the broth or broth mixture. Stir constantly. Season with salt and pepper. Pour the cream sauce over the mussels and serve.

Roasted Mussels

This is a simple camping dish that is fun to prepare. Collect and clean a quantity of mussels (full directions are found in the foraging section). Break the shell and remove the meat. Thread the mussels on a skewer or thin green stick and roast over an open fire or charcoal. A very simple meal with no clean-up required, and most tasty.

Seafood Spaghetti Sauce Using Leftover Steamed Mussels

1 cupful of mussels, steamed, picked out from shells, and chopped
1/3 cup olive oil
4 cloves garlic, pressed or finely chopped
1 cup white wine
2 cups canned tomatoes (plum tomatoes are best)
salt and pepper to taste
¼ cup chopped beach parsley (Zone III)

Cook garlic in hot oil until it begins to turn brown. Remove from the heat to cool a bit and then add the wine. Cook this mixture over high heat until it is reduced to about a half cup. Lower the heat, stir in the drained tomatoes, and heat through. Add the mussel pieces to the sauce. Taste and add salt and pepper if desired. Serve over boiled pasta with lots of chopped beach parsley.

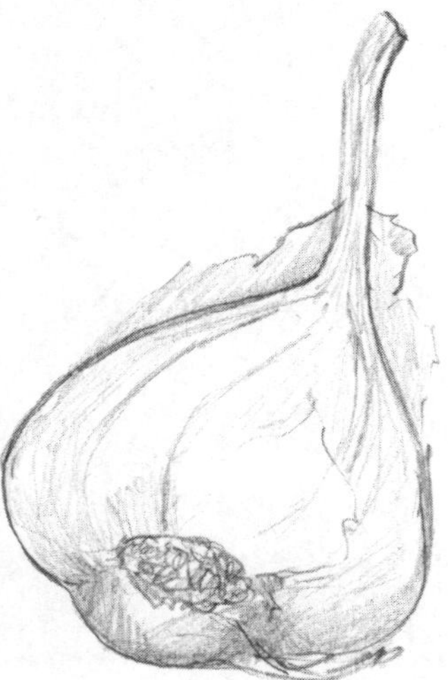

Periwinkles

Steamed Periwinkles

Bring one inch of heavily salted water to boil in a large pot that has a cover. Drop the periwinkles in this boiling water. The salt is important to help facilitate the removal of these creatures from their shells — a small dash of oil added to the water will also help. Steam them for 10 minutes; then drain, and allow them to cool a bit.

Now they have to be "picked out." This is best done with a strong hat pin, but a nut or lobster pick, even a toothpick, can be used if no hat pin can be located. After you have stuck the pin or pick into the meat, twist it gently as it unwinds itself from the shell as you pull, producing one or two pieces. The operculum or "door" should be removed by gently prying it off — it is brownish and resembles a popcorn hull. The "winkles" are now ready to be used in any of the suggested recipes, or eaten as is, perhaps dunked in some seafood or tartar sauce, or garlic butter.

Marinated Periwinkles

steamed periwinkles
olive oil
vinegar
onion slices
garlic cloves, slivered
black pepper
oregano (optional)

After the meat has been picked from the shell, place the periwinkles in a glass jar with a good lid. Add enough oil and vinegar (half and half) to come up over the meat. Then add a fair proportion of onion slices and fresh, slivered garlic. Add pepper to taste, and oregano, if desired. When you are through, shake the jar well and be certain that this pickling solution covers all. Refrigerate and shake up periodically. They'll be ready to eat in a day's time with a seafood fork, toothpick, or fingers.

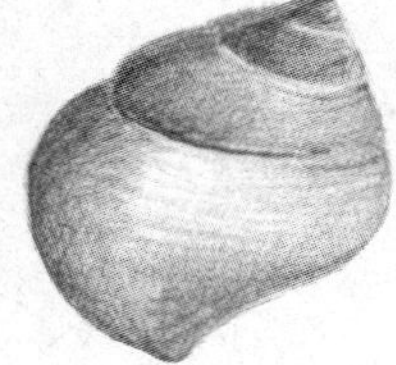

Periwinkle Spaghetti Sauce

This recipe usually appeals to people who find marinated periwinkles too chewy for their taste. It also makes a satisfying and delicious dinner from this easily foraged food.

a tomato-based spaghetti sauce of your choice (about 2 cups)
one cup chopped, steamed periwinkles
pasta, cooked

Add the chopped periwinkles to spaghetti sauce and simmer until heated through. Serve sauce on the drained pasta. Garnish with some chopped beach parsley (Zone III), some parmesan cheese, and a grating of fresh black pepper.

Sea Urchin Caviar (raw sea urchin roe)

sea urchin roe (following directions on page 19 to obtain the roe sacs)
crackers
fresh lemon juice, or Worcestershire sauce

Brace yourself, lightly wash the orange-colored roe sacs, and think of caviar — a coveted raw roe eaten the world around. Now, spread some of the urchin roe on a cracker, sprinkle with a bit of lemon juice or Worcestershire sauce, and taste. It *is* good — surprise! You may choose to add mayonnaise or chopped parsley, but just "as is" is the overall favorite.

Steamed Sea Urchin Roe

Place the roe sacs in a steamer or on a steamer rack above rapidly boiling water. Cover the pot and steam for 3 to 5 minutes. Remove cooked roe to a bowl. Mash with a fork, and add a bit of mayonnaise, some salt and pepper, and grated lemon rind. Serve on crackers or on a cucumber slice.

Roasted Sea Urchins, American Indian Style

Take freshly collected sea urchins and throw them on the coals of a campfire. Allow the spines to burn, and then remove the urchins from the coals. When they are cool enough to handle, split them open, remove the five sections of the still steaming roe, and spread it thickly on bread or crackers.

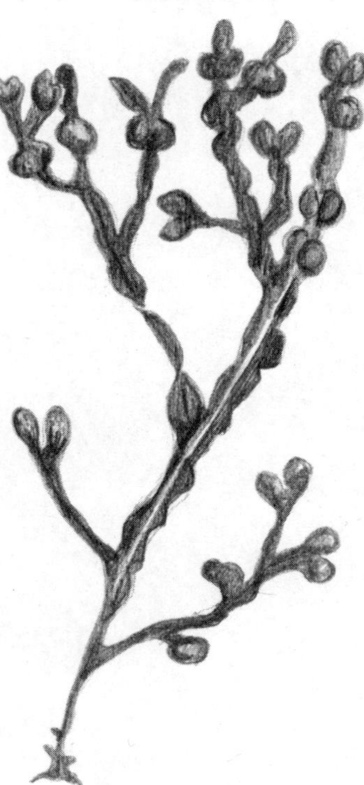

Sea Vegetables

Rockweed

Fresh rockweed makes an excellent bed for steaming seafoods and vegetables — as in traditional clambakes. When laid on hot coals on the beach or in a pot over a fire, its moisture provides the necessary steam for cooking. To steam seafood in a pot, pour in one inch of water, followed by a layer of rockweed. Whether in the open on coals or in a kettle, use enough rockweed to create a 5-inch bottom layer. Add the first layer of food; it could be potatoes, corn, onions, clams, mussels, or lobsters. Top with two inches of rockweed and continue alternating layers of food and seaweed. Finish with a final layer of seaweed, cover, and steam for about one hour, or until the foods test done. If you are steaming these foods in a pit over hot rocks and coals, cover the pile with a canvas tarpaulin to seal in the steam. After picking out the first round of servings, the hot rockweed left in the pit (or pot) tends to keep the remaining foods hot and moist.

Rockweed Tea

When you make this tea, remember that rockweed is especially high in vitamin A in the summer and vitamin C in the autumn. In general, this tea is made from rockweed that has been air- or sun-dried (or oven-dried at 100° to 150° with the door ajar), but it can also be made from fresh seaweed. Gather a quantity of rockweed, tear or cut the branches from their tough main stalks, and thoroughly wash these pieces in fresh water. Cut or chop into still smaller pieces. Add a small handful of fresh, or a teaspoon of the dried and crumbled rockweed, to a cup of boiling water. Steep for about 5 minutes. Add honey, if desired.

Rockweed as Flavoring

When preparing any seafood recipe that uses water as the main cooking medium (see Zone I recipes), be certain to add some rockweed. Rockweed gives a delicious and deep, sea-water flavor to poached or steamed seafoods. Add chunks of the seaweed to the cooking water; lift out and discard at serving time. If you are making a chowder or soup, enclose a little rockweed in a bag of doubled cheesecloth (make a square of the doubled cheese cloth, gather the corners, and tie them together). Remove the bag before serving.

Irish Moss

Since Irish moss is salty tasting and has a fairly strong sea odor, due to its high sulphur content, it must be soaked in many changes of fresh water and cooked up to a half hour (to dilute its flavor a bit). It is always cooked before eating.

These basic quantity rules are helpful to refer to when cooking with Irish moss:

½ cup dried, chopped, and packed = ½ oz.
½ cup dried, chopped, and packed = 1 cup fresh moss
These amounts will gel 1 quart of liquid

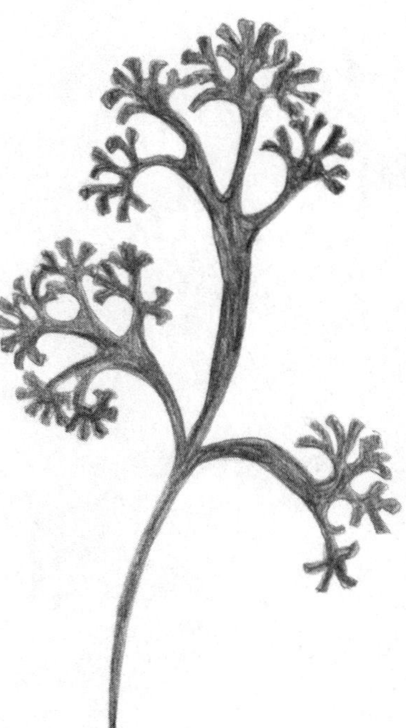

Gelled Tomato Salad

2 cups tomato juice, or 2½ cups canned or fresh tomatoes, mashed
1 cup fresh Irish moss, well washed in many changes of fresh water and soaked
1 bayberry leaf (Zone III)
up to ½ cup beach parsley, chopped (Zone III), or 1 cup chopped fresh celery
¼ cup chopped green pepper
2 tablespoons chopped onion
1 tablespoon lemon juice
1 teaspoon grated lemon rind (optional)
½ teaspoon paprika
½ teaspoon basil
salt and pepper to taste

Heat tomatoes or juice in a medium saucepan. Place Irish moss and bayberry in a large doubled square of cheesecloth. Tie up the corners and suspend this bag in the hot tomato mixture. Simmer gently, squeezing against the bag with a broad spoon and stirring the mixture often. (This will cause the gelling properties of the Irish moss to blend with the hot liquid.) After a half hour of this simmering and squeezing, remove the bag, squeeze as dry as possible, and discard its contents. Now add the chopped parsley and onion; leftover cooked fish and seafoods are wonderful additions, too. Add lemon juice, rind, and spices, and taste for salt and pepper. Without delay, pour the mixture in a dish and chill the salad a few hours, or until firm. This salad can be unmolded on a plate or scooped out of the dish. It is especially good when topped with a bit of mayonnaise.

Irish Moss Sauce for Steamed Fish (see recipes for pollack and cunner)

- 2 cups fresh milk, or reconstituted from powdered milk using fish broth as the liquid
- ½ cup fresh Irish moss, well washed in many changes of fresh water and soaked
- ¼ cup chopped onion
- 2 tablespoons butter, margarine, or oil
- salt and freshly ground pepper, to taste
- 1 teaspoon dried tarragon (optional)
- 1 egg, hard-boiled and chopped (optional)

Place Irish moss and onion in a doubled cheesecloth square, draw up and tie ends to make a bag. Suspend this in the milk and heat to the simmering point. Continue to simmer 20 minutes, watching closely to prevent the mixture from boiling at any time. Press against cheesecloth bag periodically with a broad spoon and stir the mixture often. After 20 minutes, remove the bag. Add butter, salt and pepper to taste, and any of the optional choices. Serve over hot steamed or boiled fish. Reheat leftover seafoods and serve in this warmed sauce.

Irish Moss Soup

Actually, chopped Irish moss can be added to any soup, and it will boost its nutritional value and thicken the liquid. Following is a basic soup recipe that can be altered according to the supplies on hand and the number of guests to be served.

½ cup Irish moss, well washed in many changes of fresh water and soaked for ½ hour, then chopped to a ½" to 1" mince
2 quarts fresh water
a handful of beach parsley (Zone III)
2 or 3 carrots, scrubbed and sliced
1 onion, sliced
various available vegetables: any wild potherb (Zone III), sliced mushrooms, celery, or tomatoes
1 bayberry leaf (Zone III)
2 or 3 whole peppercorns
sprinkling of thyme
soy sauce
leftover cooked rice, noodles, or sliced boiled potatoes
½ cup white wine

Place all ingredients but the rice, noodles, or potatoes and wine in a big pot. Simmer for several hours until the Irish moss is tender. Check for saltiness, adding soy sauce if desired. Now add the wine, and rice, noodles, or potatoes, and heat through. If you're using raw potatoes add them during the last half hour of cooking time. Serve hot in bowls with a garnish of chopped beach parsley.

Irish Moss Hot Lemonade

½ cup fresh Irish moss, well washed in many changes of fresh water and soaked
juice of 2 lemons
1 quart water
honey or sugar to taste

Soak Irish moss until soft in fresh water to cover. Drain and add to simmering water and cook ½ hour. Cool just a bit, then strain and add the fresh lemon juice, sweetening to taste. Serve as hot as you like. If it seems too thick, add hot water and stir briskly.

Stir-fried Irish Moss

A different and surprising vegetable course that is wonderful to serve to sceptics — they'll never know they're eating seaweed!

2 cups packed fresh Irish moss, well washed in several changes of fresh water. Soak for ½ hour, swishing occasionally to loosen any lingering sand.
2 onions, sliced

2 cloves garlic, minced
½ cup olive or vegetable oil, or a combination of both

Heat oil in a skillet and add onions and garlic; sauté slowly until limp. Drain, pat dry the seaweed, and tear or cut it into small pieces. Add to the skillet and stir-fry until tender and soft, about 10 minutes. Delicious! This recipe is also good with an additional sprinkling of soy sauce. Some prefer a crispier texture, which can be obtained through longer cooking — up to ½ hour.

Puddings

These gelled desserts are made with Irish moss and various flavorings. Storm-cast and sun-bleached Irish moss will actually produce a stiffer pudding (having developed more carrageenan) but will have fewer nutrients.

Basic Irish Moss Pudding — Blanc Mange

½ cup fresh Irish moss, thoroughly washed and swished in several changes of fresh water
1 quart milk
½ cup honey or sugar
pinch of salt
1 teaspoon vanilla (or almond extract)

After a good washing, soak the Irish moss in cold water — 10 minutes for fresh and ½ hour for dried moss (a scant ¼ cup). Place Irish moss in a doubled cheesecloth square; bring ends up to form a bag. Suspend bag in the milk that has been brought to a simmer. Continue to simmer the mixture for 30 minutes. Press against the bag with a broad spoon to help release the gelling agent. At the end of the cooking time, remove the bag, add sweetener, salt, and flavoring. Pour into a bowl or a mold that has been dipped in cool water first. Chill until set.

Chocolate- or Carob-flavored Pudding

Proceed in the same manner as for basic Irish-moss pudding. Add 2 tablespoons of pure cocoa or carob powder after the bag has been removed. Be certain to check for sweetness and add vanilla and salt. A pure chocolate candy bar can be broken up and added instead of the cocoa, but use less sweetener in that case.

Coffee-flavored Pudding

Add 1 to 2 teaspoons of instant coffee (to taste) or 1 cup strong coffee for 1 cup of the milk in the basic Irish moss pudding recipe.

Apple Pudding

Add 1 or 1½ cups of chopped apple pieces (Zone III) and 1 tablespoon lemon juice to the basic Irish moss pudding mixture after the bag is removed. Pour into a mold and cover with foil. This should have a few hours to set.

Edible Kelp — Alaria

Note: If using dried alaria, be certain to soak it overnight, in fresh water, before cooking.

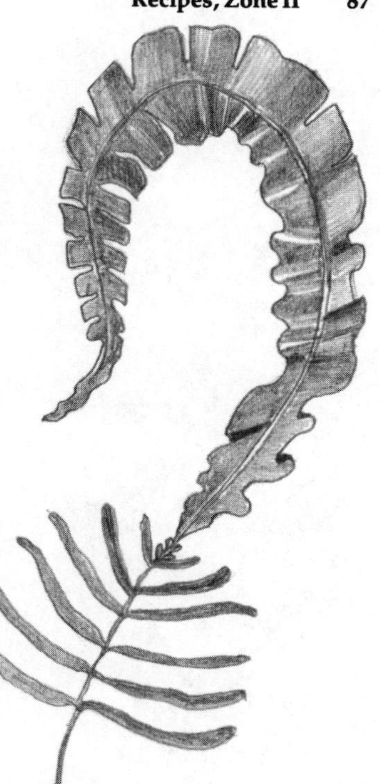

Midrib Munch

Cut away the curled edge of a fresh main frond and make short strips of the remaining rib — to resemble carrot sticks. Munch them as is, or use with a favorite dip. This kelp is mild and sweet to the taste — a nice surprise.

Kelp and Co. Salad

fresh alaria midribs, washed
wild greens (Zone III) in any amount or combination
onion slices, carrots, etc.
salad dressing

Take slices of fresh alaria midrib prepared as in Midrib Munch, above, and toss with the other suggested ingredients. Depending on the additions, this salad is hardy and easy to make.

Alaria Soup

These are basic starter ingredients; any suitable leftovers, including cooked fish and canned vegetables, can be added.

1 cup washed, fresh, alaria (or ½ cup dried and soaked overnight) cut across the frond into 1" strips

2 tablespoons oil
2 quarts water, to start
1 handful beach parsley (Zone III)
1 bayberry leaf (Zone III)
1 teaspoon basil
2 cups soup vegetables: sliced carrots, onions, celery, etc.
beach peas (whole pods in June, shelled peas in early summer) (Zone III)
1 cup cooked rice
soy sauce

Heat oil in a skillet and sauté the alaria for five minutes or so. Then place in a soup pot, with the water. (Use the soaking water if dried Alaria is used.) Boil gently, uncovered, for one hour. Check water level and add more to keep the alaria well covered. Now cover the pot and cook for another two hours. Add bayberry leaf, basil, and raw vegetables. Cover and gently boil for 45 minutes. Add cooked rice and heat. Check for seasonings, adding a dash or two of soy sauce. Serve hot.

Kelp Stew

1 cup washed, fresh, alaria (or ½ cup dried and reconstituted) cut across the fronds into 1″ strips
2 medium onions, sliced
2 cloves garlic, minced
1 bayberry leaf (Zone III)
1 cup water
2 or 3 potatoes, washed and cut into chunks (skin on)

4 or 5 carrots, sliced thickly
1 small can tomatoes with juice or 3 fresh tomatoes, peeled
beach peas (whole pods in June, shelled peas in early summer)
beach parsley, several stalks (Zone III)
foraged greens, mixed (Zone III)
1 cup corn kernels (optional)
1 tablespoon grated fresh ginger (optional)
½ teaspoon oregano
salt and freshly ground pepper

In a good-size pot, sauté the strips of alaria in the oil, together with the sliced onion and minced garlic, for five minutes or until the onions are limp. Cool a bit, then add the cup of water and bayberry leaf. Boil gently for two hours or so. Add the vegetables, foraged greens, and the additional spices, adding more water to the stew as needed. Simmer covered ½ hour or until the potatoes test done. Check seasonings and serve.

Stir-fried Alaria

This dish can only be made in the month of June when alaria kelp is young and delicate.

2 cups alaria, washed and cut across the fronds in 1″ strips
½ cup water
2 tablespoons oil
1 medium onion, sliced
1 clove garlic, minced
¼ cup soy sauce

In a covered skillet or wok, steam the alaria in gently boiling water until the kelp is tender. Pour out the water and drain the alaria. Heat the oil in the same skillet or wok and add the drained alaria, onion, and garlic. Lightly fry while stirring. When the onions are golden, add the soy sauce. Serve with a bit of lemon juice sprinkled on top. This dish is excellent with rice.

Clams

Steamed Clams

Besides using clams in a traditional clambake, the other favored way of cooking them is by steaming. The procedure is much like that used when steaming mussels. Live (tightly shut) clams are scrubbed and put into several changes of fresh water. A handful of cornmeal can be added to the last water and left for 15 minutes; this is optional but is a good way to get bivalves like clams and mussels to clean themselves. Steam those that remain shut, with some rockweed for additional flavor, in or above an inch or two of boiling water. Use a deep pot with a close-fitting cover. Allow one quart of clams or 20 good-sized clams per person. Cook over low heat, just maintaining the steam, for 6 to 15 minutes, until the clams barely begin to open. Do not overcook. Discard all unopened ones. Serve with hot drawn butter, with lemon juice or vinegar, if wished. You can give each diner a bowlful of the broth from the cooking pot for rinsing the clams before dunking them in the butter. The broth is also very tasty to sip.

After enough have been eaten, any leftovers can be refrigerated for later use. Left in their shells, clams can be reheated by a quick steaming. Or, pick out the meat and use it in the following recipes.

Recipes for Leftover Clam Meat

Clam Dip (for vegetables or crackers)

up to 1 cup cooked, chopped clams
1 cup of cottage cheese or sour cream, or 8 ounces cream cheese
1 minced clove of fresh garlic (optional)
⅛ teaspoon thyme
1 teaspoon finely chopped beach parsley
¼ teaspoon salt (optional)
dash of hot pepper sauce (optional)

Combine clams with the chosen dairy product and then blend in the other ingredients. If too stiff to dip into, thin out with some sherry, milk, or cream.

Quick Clam Chowder

1 to 2 cups leftover shucked clams
small piece of salt pork, minced (1″ to 2″ cube)
1 medium onion, chopped
1 cup cubed potato (skin can be left on)
2½ cups boiling water

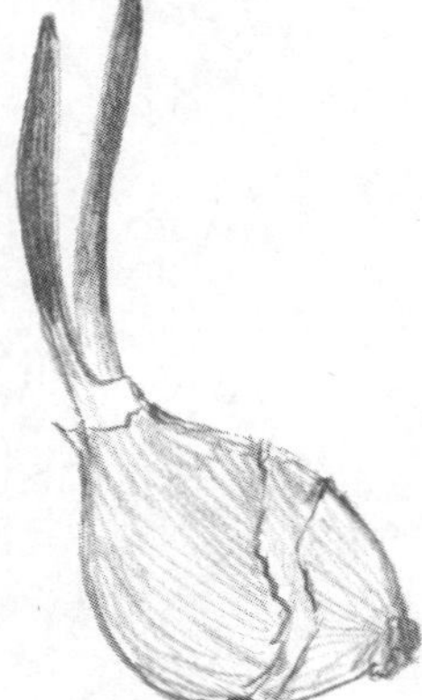

1 chicken bouillon cube (optional)
¼ teaspoon thyme
1 13 oz. can evaporated milk, or 1½ cups whole milk
3 tablespoons butter or margarine
salt, pepper, and paprika to taste
chopped beach parsley (optional)

In a large pot, slowly fry the minced salt pork until it is crisp and brown. Remove the "tried out" brown bits and set them aside. Cook the onion pieces in the remaining fat until transparent, then slowly add the potatoes, boiling water, bouillon cube, and thyme. Simmer for 20 minutes. Add the chopped clams and heat through. Now add the evaporated milk (or whole milk), butter, and seasonings. Heat through, but do not allow to boil. This can be made ahead and stored a day or two to develop flavor, or it can be served right away. When ladled into bowls, sprinkle some crisp pork scraps on top of each, and some chopped beach parsley.

Clam Fritters

1 cup or so of cooked, chopped clams
2 eggs, beaten
½ cup flour (or ¾ cup cracker crumbs — traditional), more if needed
½ teaspoon baking powder
1 tablespoon finely chopped onion
½ teaspoon salt, and some pepper
oil, for pan frying

Stir all ingredients in a bowl. If mixture will not hold together, add a bit more flour or cracker crumbs, but if it's too dry, add a tablespoon of milk at a time, and stir until moist enough. Heat about ¼ cup oil in a large skillet until it begins to smoke. Carefully drop the fritter mixture into the oil by large spoonfuls. Flatten each one a bit so it will be of a uniform thickness. Fry 2 or 3 minutes on each side until nicely browned. Do not overcook as the fritters will get tough. Makes 10 big cakes.

Clam Newburg

Clams can be served in the same Newburg sauce that is made for lobster. In fact, several seafoods can be combined, as available, to produce a rich seafood newburg. (Consult lobster recipes, (Page 68.)

Zone III

The Shoreline — by Seasons

Spring and Early Summer

Spring Greens

(Dandelion, wild lettuce, sow thistle, chickweed, orach and lamb's quarters, curled dock, and mustard)

In early spring — May and June — the stems and leaves of these plants can be served raw in salads and cooked as potherbs. They can be combined with each other or can augment regular lettuce and vegetable dishes. For the following recipes, use any of these greens interchangeably, according to your supply.

Note: Chickweed is so tender that it should be added at the end of any cooking period.

Wild Greens Salad

a bowlful of well-washed and drained early spring greens, torn into serving size
lettuce (optional)
½ cup olive oil or 8 slices of bacon
2 cloves garlic, minced
¼ cup vinegar (wine vinegar is preferred)
½ onion, sliced (optional)
salt and pepper
croutons (optional)

Heat olive oil in a skillet. If using bacon, fry it until crisp. Leave the fat in the skillet, but remove the bacon and save. Add the garlic to the hot oil or fat, stir, and then remove from heat. Add the vinegar and stir, scraping up whatever adheres to the pan's bottom. Let cool. Place greens (and onions) into the serving bowl and pour the skillet mixture over all. Add the crumbled cooked bacon, salt and pepper to taste, and the croutons.

Greens and Potatoes

a large covered potful of well-washed greens, mixed or of one variety (dandelions preferred)
½ to 1 pound of diced salt pork
water
4 or 5 large unpeeled potatoes, scrubbed and cut up

Pour water into a pot of prepared greens until it reaches 1/3 their depth. Add diced salt pork and cook covered until the greens become soft, about 10 minutes. Add the cut-up potatoes and stir. Check to make certain that there is still water in the pot and cook until the potatoes test done. Serve the greens and potatoes with a little of the "pot liquor" and possibly a sprinkling of vinegar.

Spring Stew

a potful of washed wild greens in any combination
water
1¾ cups canned tomatoes (and liquid) or tomato juice
2 or 3 onions, coarsely chopped
2 cloves garlic, minced (optional)
1 tablespoon grated fresh ginger (optional)
1 teaspoon basil or oregano
2 bayberry leaves (Zone III)
handful of beach parsley (Zone III)
1 cup very young beach pea pods or whatever you can pick
¼ cup soaked and well-washed Irish moss (Zone II), torn into small pieces (optional)
3 or 4 potatoes, cut up, or 2 cups cooked rice or pasta
soy sauce, to taste

Add water to the pot of greens until it reaches 1/3 their depth. Boil 10 minutes and then add all other ingredients. (If you're using cooked rice or pasta, add them at the end with the seasonings.) Simmer, covered, for ½ hour. Add soy sauce and check for seasonings.

Pan-fried Dandelion Buds

2 cups unopened dandelion buds, washed and drained, with stems removed
¼ cup vegetable oil
½ onion, sliced (optional)
salt and pepper to taste

Heat oil and onion slices in a skillet until onions turn limp. Add a few buds to cover half the pan and fry until they pop open. Remove to absorbent paper and continue to fry the buds until all are cooked. Drain remaining oil, if any, and return the fried buds to the skillet for a quick reheating; stir constantly. Add salt and pepper, if desired.

Creamed Orach, Lamb's Quarters, Curled Dock, or Mustard

potful of well-washed greens
1 cup onion slices
water
½ cup sour cream or yogurt
nutmeg to taste
salt and pepper
2 or 3 strips crumbled, cooked bacon (optional)

Add sliced onions to the pot of greens and pour in water to 1/3 the depth of the greens. Boil, covered, until tender (about 10 minutes). Drain well and stir in the sour cream or yogurt and a few gratings of

nutmeg. Taste to see if salt and pepper are needed. Serve immediately, while hot, or reheat very slowly, stirring all the while. Sprinkle servings with crumbled bacon.

Mustard and/or Curled Dock in a Cheese Sauce

potful of mustard greens and/or curled dock, well washed
water
1 chopped onion
4 tablespoons butter, margarine or oil
2 cups milk, whole or reconstituted
1 cup grated cheddar cheese
2 teaspoons paprika
salt and pepper

Add water to half the level of the greens in the pot; add onion. Cover pot and cook until greens test done (10 minutes or so). Drain well into a strainer. Make a cream sauce by melting the butter in the same pot. Add the flour and blend into a smooth paste. Slowly pour in the milk, stirring constantly. Add the grated cheese, a handful at a time. Stir until smooth. Sprinkle in the paprika, and the salt and pepper if necessary. Return the drained greens and onions to the pot and stir in the cheese sauce. Heat very slowly, while stirring.

Stir-fried Beach Pea Pods and Mushrooms

1½ to 2 cups fresh, young, bright green beach pea pods with only tiny peas within
water for steaming
3 tablespoons oil
1 small can sliced mushrooms, drained, or ¼ pound fresh mushrooms
soy sauce, to taste

Steam the young beach pea pods for two or three minutes in 1″ of water in a covered pot, or in a steamer basket above the water. Heat oil in a skillet or wok, add garlic, mushrooms, and steamed pea pods and sauté three minutes, stirring all the while. Pour in soy sauce and heat two minutes more. Serve on rice.

Note: Boneless pieces of leftover fish are excellent last-minute additions to this stir-fry.

Strawberries

It does not seem that recipes for wild strawberries are ever needed. The berries seldom make it back to the eating table — they are usually consumed en route. Nonetheless, keep in mind how delicious a cupful would be added to Irish moss pudding (Zone II) or to any other cut-up fresh fruits. If you do pick enough, use them for such favorites as strawberry shortcake, tarts, or strawberry sauce for desserts and pancakes. Strawberries are always superb additions to dry granola breakfasts. May you pick and enjoy lots of them.

Summer

Summer Greens

(Dandelion, wild lettuce, sow thistle, orach, lamb's quarters, chickweed, mustard, sea rocket, goosetongue, and beach parsley)

Summer means that the more mature spring greens should be treated as cooked potherbs now. Throw off the first cooking water and bring to a boil a second time in fresh water. This will dilute their slightly bitter summer flavor. For potherb recipes, refer to spring and early summer greens recipes (pages 94–98).

Potato or Macaroni Salad with Mustard Blossoms

Prepare your favorite potato or macaroni salad and add ½ cup or so of mustard blossoms before the final blending. They make a tasty and attractive addition.

Boiled Sea Rocket

2 cups washed sea rocket stems, leaves, and flower heads, cut up
1 onion, sliced (optional)
water
salt and pepper
butter

Place the cut-up sea rocket in a pot, add the onion, and an inch or so of water to the pot. Cover and bring to a boil. Cook 15 to 20 minutes, or until tender. Drain, season, and serve with butter.

Sea Rocket in Sandwiches

Add crunchy sprigs of fresh sea rocket instead of lettuce to sandwiches. It's elegant with egg salad, tuna, leftover cooked fish, sliced meat, or meat spread, sliced tomatoes, and other cold vegetables. It adds a special pungency.

Goosetongue — Boiled, Buttered, and Simple

Prepare cut-up goosetongue stalks as for boiled sea rocket (Page 100).

Creamed Beach Parsley

1½ cups chopped beach parsley (Zone III) stems with the leaves removed
1 onion, sliced
water
2 tablespoons butter, margarine, or oil
2 tablespoons flour
1 cup milk, whole or reconstituted powdered milk
1 teaspoon thyme or chopped mint leaves (Zone III)

Place the chopped stems, stalks, and onion slices into a little water and boil three to five minutes until tender. Drain off water. Make a standard cream sauce by melting the butter in a large pot. Add the

flour and blend into a smooth paste. Slowly pour in the milk, stirring constantly. Add drained beach parsley and onion, and the thyme or mint. Stir and serve.

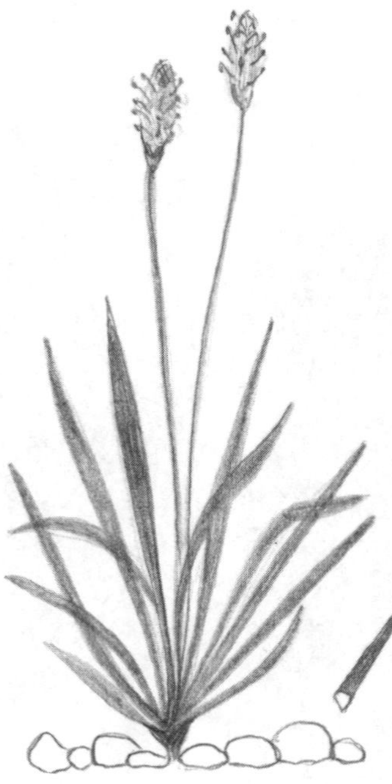

Summer Bounty Salad

bowlful of assorted tender greens (washed and dried): include beach parsley, goosetongue, sea rocket, some chickweed, and new orach growth
½ onion, sliced thinly
1 carrot, shredded or finely chopped
leftover cooked vegetables (optional)
handful of croutons (optional)
½ cup cheese, cut into cubes (optional)
½ cup olive oil
scant ¼ cup wine vinegar
2 tablespoons soy sauce
½ teaspoon oregano
1 teaspoon honey or sugar (optional)
salt and pepper to taste
½ cup mustard blossoms

Wash and prepare all greens and vegetables. Dry, and add to salad bowl. Toss first with the oil, then add the other ingredients (except the mustard blossoms). Gently toss until all is well blended. Sprinkle mustard blossoms on top of salad and serve.

Beach Peas

1 cup fresh green peas, lovingly shelled from bright green pods
½ onion, sliced
½ cup reconstituted powdered milk or water
butter
2 to 3 teaspoons finely chopped fresh mint leaves (optional)
freshly ground black pepper

Boil the peas and onions in the milk or water for a few minutes, until tender. Drain, add butter, chopped mint, and freshly ground black pepper. Serve by the spoonful. You can augment the portions by adding a cup of cream sauce and ¼ cup of chopped beach parsley.

Mint

Mint Tea, Hot or Cold

for one serving:
1 or 2 sprigs of fresh mint, washed
1 cup boiling water

Pour boiling water into a cup over the mint. (Pour the water over a spoon, if you're using a glass, to prevent its cracking.) Steep for five to seven minutes. If desired, sweeten with honey. Served in a glass, this greenish tea is especially appealing. For a cold drink, let cool and add ice.

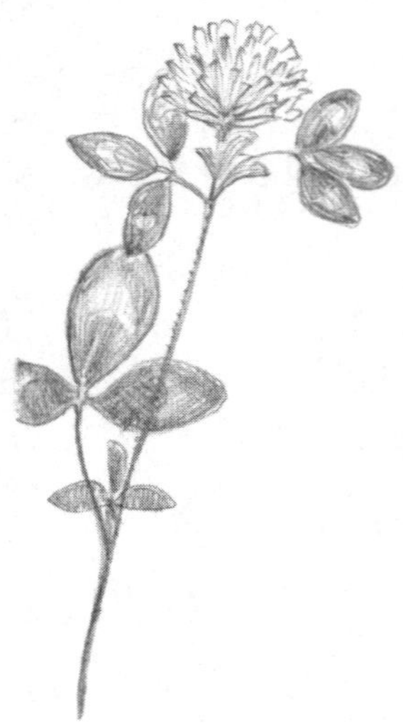

Carrots with Mint

After cooking fresh carrots, drain them, and add some chopped mint leaves, butter, and coarsely ground black pepper for an easy taste treat.

Note: Try using some chopped mint on top of a cold, leftover vegetable salad. Toss with dressing.

Red Clover

Red Clover Tea with Mint — or Alone

Brew this tea as you would the mint tea described previously. Add a few blossoms of red clover to the mint stalks or brew the tea solely from red clover blossoms. Sweeten with honey, if desired.

Bayberry Leaves

Use in recipes calling for bayberry.

Berries — Blueberries, Raspberries, and Blackberries

It is rare when enough berries for a pie or turnovers (usually four cups) are brought back from an outing or even enough to go on shortcake or in muffins (two cups). Besides, an oven is required for these treats. But a few berries added to the batter make awfully good pancakes, which need only a griddle or a skillet, and they're very special on top of cold cereal. If you do gather a large quantity, cook them up in jams and jellies.

On a vacation, the simplest way to enjoy freshly picked berries is topped with a dollop of sour cream or yogurt (plain or fruited). These berries combine well with each other and with other fruits such as bananas, apples, peaches, etc. A little orange juice and honey binds all together, and a little bit of chopped fresh mint is a delicious addition.

Note: Raspberry leaves can be brewed for tea, alone or in combination with mint. Consult mint tea recipe, page 103.

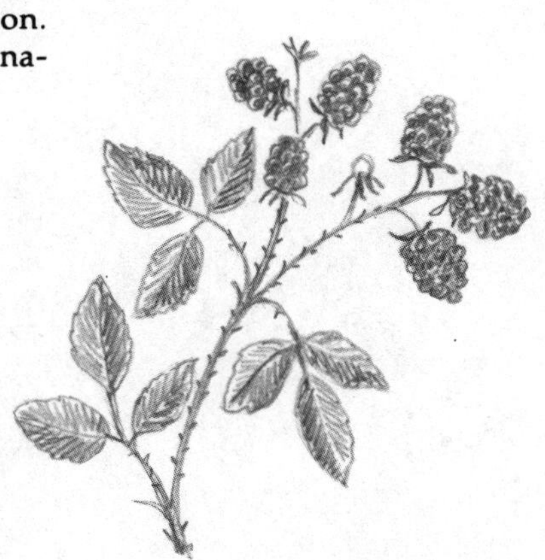

Late Summer and Autumn

Apples

Sautéed Apples and Onions

1½ cups cut-up apple pieces
1 cup onion, coarsely chopped
½ cup beach parsley leaves and stems, chopped
¼ cup water
2 tablespoons oil, more if needed

Place apple and onion pieces in a skillet with the chopped beach parsley and water. Cover skillet (with foil or a plate if no top is available) and steam gently for 10 minutes. Remove from heat. When cool, add oil and sauté the mixture, stirring gently. Cook until some of the liquid has evaporated and serve as a vegetable. If you have some, caraway seeds add a nice flavor.

Stewed Apples

2 cups apple chunks
2 sticks cinnamon or 1 teaspoon ground cinnamon
½ to 1 cup rose hips, seeded and chopped (optional)
water
honey or sugar (optional)

Put the apple chunks in a pot. (Leave on the unsprayed skins if you wish; they add a lovely color.) Add the cinnamon and rose hips; pour in water until it is barely visible through the apples. Cover, and simmer ½ hour on a low flame. Add honey or sugar to taste and stew for ½ hour more. Serve warm or cold, plain, or with a bit of sour cream.

Apple Salad

2 cups chopped washed apples with skins
½ cup raisins
¼ cup beach parsley stems and stalks, chopped
2 tablespoons finely chopped mint leaves
¼ cup chopped walnuts
mayonnaise and yogurt, or sour cream

Place fruit and vegetables in a bowl. Bind with mayonnaise and yogurt, or sour cream, until blended. Serve as a side dish or as a dessert.

Rose Hips

Note: Do not use copper or aluminum cooking or stirring equipment when picking or preparing rose hips.

Cold Rose Hip Soup

3 cups fresh, whole rose hips
1 cinnamon stick, broken up, or ¼ teaspoon ground cinnamon
1½ quarts water
1½ tablespoons cornstarch
½ cup honey or sugar

Drop rose hips and cinnamon into boiling water. Cover pot and boil until tender. Using a wooden spoon, press the cooked mass through a food mill or sieve. Measure the pulp and add water to make 1½ quarts. Return the mixture to the stove, add honey or sugar. Make a paste with the cornstarch and a bit of cold water; add to the pulp mixture. Bring to a boil, and stir with a wooden spoon until the soup turns clear. Let cool, and then chill. Serve in bowls with a dollop of sour cream.

Rose Hip Tea

Cut rose hips into quarters, spread them in a single layer, and air dry in the sun (or use an oven set at 100° to 150°, with the door ajar). To make tea, chop up 1 or 2 tablespoons of dried rose hips for each cup and place in a teapot. Pour in boiling water and let brew five minutes, then strain into a cup.

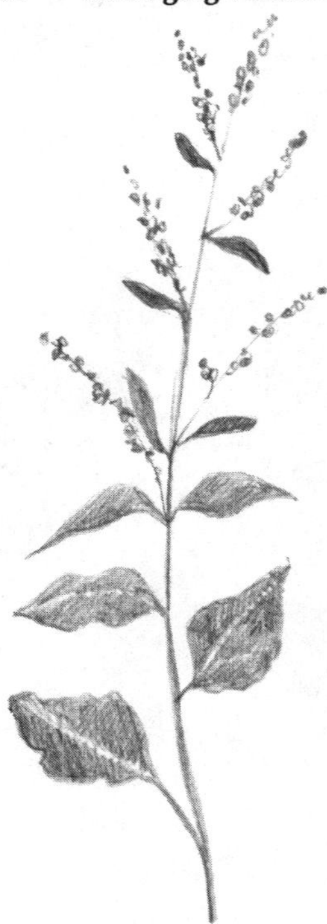

Cinnamon Rose Tea

Follow directions for rose hip tea and add a 1" piece of cinnamon stick (or pinch of ground cinnamon) per serving.

Rose Hip Syrup

2 cups rose hips, washed and cut up
2 sticks cinnamon (optional)
water
honey

In a pot, barely cover the cut-up rose hips with water; add cinnamon and simmer until soft. Using a double thickness of cheesecloth (not a metal sieve), pour off the liquid and reserve. Repeat this process again with just enough water to barely cover the rose hip mash. Simmer 15 to 20 minutes and again pour off the liquid, using cheesecloth as a strainer. Combine the second batch of liquid with the first. Measure the volume and for each cup of juice, add ¾ cup of honey. Simmer until the liquid thickens a bit. Store in the refrigerator, or seal in sterilized jars. Rose hip syrup is marvelous over pancakes, waffles, and desserts.

Autumn Greens

(Seaside lamb's quarters, chickweed, curled dock, and beach parsley)

You can pick the new growth of these hardy greens well into autumn. Boil them up and use them in the recipes for cooked potherbs in the spring and summer listings. Since they're more bitter at this time of year than earlier in the season, you'll want to cook them in two changes of water. Discard the water in which they're first boiled, add fresh water, and return to a boil. Pieces of salt pork, cooked with the greens, are a welcome addition.

Sea Rocket Seed Pods, Plain or with Apples

1½ to 2 cups sea rocket seed pods
1 cup apple chunks (optional)
2 or 3 onions, coarsely chopped
water
salt and pepper to taste

Add all of the ingredients except for salt and pepper to a pot. Pour in water until it's just visible through the food. Cover, and cook for ½ hour. Stir occasionally. When tender, add salt, if needed, and add freshly ground black pepper. Serve with butter.

Dried Beach Pea Soup

Follow any recipe for dried-pea soup and force the tiny cooked peas through a mill or sieve to remove the coarse hulls. Season with thyme, salt, and pepper, and thin with milk, if necessary.

Items to Bring Along

Although simplicity has been a theme throughout this book, there are some special things to be considered when preparing for your foraging adventure. Following is a list of the staples, seasonings, and equipment you will need to make the recipes in this book. Foods and seasonings noted as "optional" in the recipes are listed separately.

Produce

onions
garlic, cloves
carrots
potatoes
celery
cucumbers
green pepper
mushrooms, fresh or canned
tomatoes, fresh or canned (plum best)
canned beans, limas, kidney, chickpeas
parsley, fresh or dried

Herbs and Spices

basil
dillweed
thyme
tarragon
paprika
oregano
garlic powder
dry mustard
salt
black peppercorns, whole
pure vanilla, or almond extract
cinnamon, sticks and/or ground

Dairy, eggs, etc.

milk, fresh, powdered, skimmed, and evaporated
eggs
butter / margarine
yogurt / sour cream
cheddar cheese

Sundries and Extras

raisins
nuts (walnuts are good)
honey or sugar
flour
cornstarch

dry cereal (granola)
corn meal, cracker or bread crumbs
vegetable oil
olive oil
vinegar, cider or red wine
soy sauce
lemon juice (fresh or bottled)
chili sauce
horseradish
Tabasco (hot) sauce
ketchup
chicken bouillon cubes

Liquids

tomato juice
dry white wine for cooking
dry sherry for cooking

Fishing Equipment

rod, or drop line
sinkers
bucket
knife (fillet one is best)
dip net (optional)
old sneakers, "flip flops"
cotton work gloves
tide calendar
compass
diamond jigs
small hooks, size #1/0 to #3/0
scrub brush, for mussels

Cooking Equipment

big soup or steamer pot with cover
frying pan
saucepans
bowls, assorted
wooden spoon
slotted, pierced spoon
metal spatula/turner
long fork, or tongs
steamer rack (optional)
large sieve or strainer
basting brush
pepper mill
hibachi with racks and charcoal (optional)
food mill (optional)
aluminum foil
assorted plastic bags
cheesecloth
lobster/seafood cracker and picks
a strong hat pin for periwinkles
scissors
knives (and sharpening stone)
skewers (optional)
garlic press (optional)
drawstring mesh bag (optional)
fine-mesh grater

Optional Food Items for Specialized Recipes

sesame seeds (fishcakes)
stuffed olives (Mexican fish stew)
canned chopped green chili peppers (seviche)
avocado (seviche)
limes (6) (seviche)
saffron (paella, Mediterranean sopa)
seafood seasoning (boiling crabs)
salt pork (chowder, greens)
bacon (salads, greens)
canned corn (chowder, kelp stew)
fresh ginger (many fish dishes, kelp stew, spring stew with greens)
chunk pineapple (crabmeat salad)
carob or cocoa powder (puddings)
cream cheese (clam dip)

Books to Bring Along

Green Island, Green Sea, Philip Conkling
Stalking the Blue-Eyed Scallop, Euell Gibbons
Stalking the Healthful Herbs, Euell Gibbons
the seavegetable book, Judith Cooper Madlener

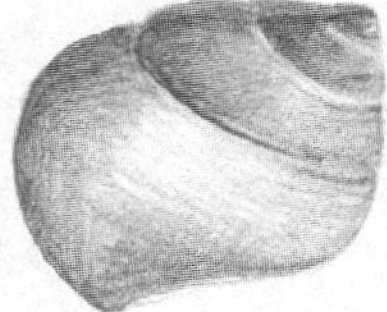

Meal Accompaniments

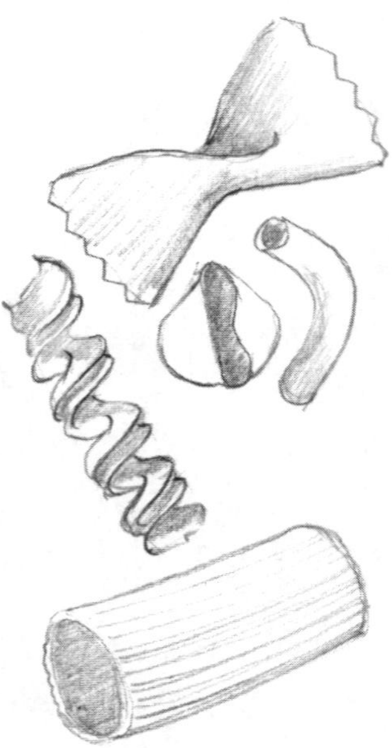

Following is a list of some food staples that are easy to store and prepare. They will augment your foraged foods and turn them into full meals, even if your vacation kitchen has only minimal cooking equipment. May these suggestions spur all sorts of variations and fresh ideas.

Grains

Store grains in capped jars or containers. Once cooked they will keep a day at 60° or 70°, if not prepared with eggs or dairy products.

Rice is a versatile accompaniment to seafood meals. As it doubles in volume once cooked, rice is a compact and economical grain. Brown rice is especially nutritious, although converted white rice is also desirable and cooks more quickly. It is wise to prepare more rice than you need, for one meal; it stores well at room temperature for a day and can be added to soups, stews, and even salads.

Different kinds of pasta are also handy to bring along; their cooking time is short and they also double in volume once cooked. The most convenient and fastest-cooking pastas are thin spaghetti, linguini, and vermicelli. Shells, macaroni, ziti, and bows also travel well.

Couscous is a Mediterranean grain that deserves attention. It cooks quickly; add it to a double measure of boiling water with a chicken bouillon cube, cover and remove from the heat. Let it sit for 20 minutes. To serve, fluff the couscous with a fork. Add butter and some salt, if desired, and top with sautéed vegetables.

Bulghur is another form of wheat that cooks rather quickly. Stir it into a double measure of boiling water with a chicken bouillon cube (optional), and simmer covered for 15 to 20 minutes. It can be eaten even sooner if you're in a hurry, once it has absorbed the boiling water. Add sautéed onion, garlic, or green pepper and you have a hearty dish.

Assorted whole-grain crackers make a simple and nutritious complement to your meals. The Scandinavian large rectangular ones are especially good. They should be stored in airtight containers if you're near salt water.

Bread sticks are a cross between bread and crackers and they keep very well. They go well with cold dishes and salads.

Vegetables

Keep a small bag of potatoes at hand to use in soups and chowders, or to serve with boiled wild greens. They store well in cool, though not refrigerated, spots.

Carrots are an excellent vegetable to bring along; they store well in a cool place and can be prepared in a variety of ways. Some tried and true methods of serving them: raw — cut into sticks or diagonal slices and served with a dip; or as a salad, grated and tossed with celery seeds, oil and vinegar, or mayonnaise, and raisins or nuts; and cooked — only until crisp-tender by steaming, boiling or stir-frying, with spices or herbs added, as desired.

Squashes — zucchini, yellow, or the like — also store easily and require a short cooking period. Basil and black pepper go well with summer squashes.

Assorted raw vegetables should not be overlooked in this simplified cooking venture. There are the regulars: washed and cut-up celery, cucumbers, and green peppers. And there are many other vegetables that can be served raw, depending upon their availability: raw zucchini slices, whole or cut-up mushrooms, small sections of broccoli and cauliflower, or wonderfully sweet, crisp slices of uncooked turnip. Of course sliced tomatoes or little cherry tomatoes are always available and tasty in summer months.

Most salad greens are a bit touchy due to their delicate storage requirements, but they will keep for short periods of time. Cabbage is more dependable and can be used in slaws and salads, raw, and steamed or boiled just until limp. Dillweed is a wonderful herb to add to cabbage dishes. For storage, the head of cabbage can be placed in a plastic bag or a sealed container and kept in a cool spot. In time, you may lose a few outer leaves, but if used in two weeks or so, those inside will be fresh and good.

Cheeses and desserts

Hard cheeses — cheddar, provolone, swiss, monterey jack, edam, and gouda — are the best "keepers" in a vacation setup. One or two chunks of uncut cheeses, wrapped in foil and kept in the coolest spot (while not necessarily refrigerated), would be grand to have on hand as additions to meals. They may harden on the edges, but this can be grated on top of vegetables and salads and incorporated into cooked foods as extra protein boosts. And cheese makes a nice ending to meals, perhaps combined with fresh fruit and crackers.

For easy-to-store desserts, other than foraged fruits, bring along soft cookies (crisp varieties will wilt), bars, honey cake, and fruit cake. Perhaps you have a fruit cake that has been mellowing since last Christmas! Any of these desserts topped off with a mug of fresh mint tea make a very pleasant way to end a meal.

Some Final Thoughts

What seas what shores what grey rocks and what islands
What water lapping the bow
And scent of pine and the woodthrush singing through the fog
What images return . . .

"Marina"
T.S. Eliot

It is my fond hope that the pleasures of foraging have been presented strongly enough to have intrigued new members into this interdependent fellowship. Everything about this sort of endeavor is pleasant: the anticipation of the search, the time spent amidst this natural beauty, the joy at the point of discovery, and the pleasures from the tastes of these foods. And as the days of a vacation draw to a close, the images can be recalled, having been heightened by joyous, living experiences. Under these conditions, it is not at all difficult to claim a greater fellowship — touching life with all of nature.

Monhegan Island

Raquel Davenport Boehmer

Resources and State Agencies

For information and updated reports on closed tidal flats and Red Tide areas, contact:

(1) The local marine patrol officer (check with the city or town manager's office for name and number).

(2) Department of Marine Resources
Bureau of Marine Patrol
98 Winthrop St.
Hallowell, ME 04347
(207) 289-2291

(3) Department of Marine Resources
Boothbay Research Laboratory
Boothbay Harbor, ME 04538
(207) 633-5572

For information on state boat launching sites and state park regulations, contact:

Department of Conservation
Bureau of Parks and Recreation
State House Station 19
Augusta, ME 04333
(Attn: Mr. Ed Beach, Superintendent of Management)
(207) 289-2211

For information about restricted coastal wildlife management areas and nesting islands from May 1 through July 15, contact:

Department of Inland Fisheries and Wildlife
Wildlife Division
236 Nutting Hall
University of Maine
Orono, ME 04469
(207) 581-2506

For information on small boat rentals, campgrounds, public showers, cabins, etc.:

(1) *The Rand McNally Campground & Trailer Park Guide (Northeastern Region).* Available in bookstores, or from Rand McNally & Co., Trade Division, P.O. Box 7600, Chicago, IL 60680.

(2) *Woodall's Eastern Campground Directory.* Available in bookstores, or from Simon & Schuster Order Department, 1230 Ave. of the Americas, New York, NY 10020.

(3) *1982 State O' Maine Facts (15th edition).* Available in stores, or from Down East Books, P.O. Box 679, Camden, ME 04843.

(4) Check with the local chamber of commerce in specific coastal towns.

Bibliography

Angier, Bradford. *Field Guide to Edible Wild Plants.* Harrisburg, Pa.: Stackpole Books, 1974.

Carson, Rachel. *The Edge of the Sea.* Boston: Houghton Mifflin, 1955.

Conkling, Philip. *Green Island, Green Sea.* Rockland, Me.: Hurricane Island Outward Bound School, 1980.

Coon, Nelson. *Using Wayside Plants.* New York: Hearthside Press, 1957.

Crow, Garrett E., and Fralick, Richard A. *Edible Wild Plants of New Hampshire.* Durham: Univ. of New Hampshire, 1981.

Gibbons, Euell. *Stalking the Wild Asparagus.* New York: David McKay, 1962.

Gibbons, Euell. *Stalking the Blue-Eyed Scallop.* New York: David McKay, 1964.

Gibbons, Euell. *Stalking the Healthful Herbs.* New York: David McKay, 1966.

Gibbons, Euell. *A Wild Way to Eat.* Rockland, Me.: Hurricane Island Outward Bound School, 1967.

Gosner, Kenneth L. *A Field Guide to the Atlantic Seashore.* Boston: Houghton Mifflin, 1979.

Madlener, Judith Cooper. *the seavegetable book.* New York: Clarkson N. Potter, 1977.

Rhoads, Sharon Ann. *Cooking with Sea Vegetables.* Brookline, Ma.: Autumn Press, 1978.

Scharff, Robert. *Standard Handbook of Salt-Water Fishing.* New York: Thomas Y. Crowell, 1959.

Index

Alaria, *See* Edible Kelp
Angelica, 34
Apples. *See* Wild Apples
Atlantic Mackerel. *See* Mackerel
Bayberry Leaves. (*Myrica pensylvanica*), 36
  Alaria Soup, 87–88
  Crabmeat Bisque, 64
  Fish Stock (Court Bouillon), 54
  Gelled Tomato Salad, 81
  Irish Moss Soup, 83
  Kelp Stew, 88
  with Lobster, 70
  with Scallops, 72
  Spring Stew, 96
  Steamed Mussels, 73
Beach Celery. *See* Beach Parsley
Beach Parsley (*Ligusticus scothicum*), 33–34, 40–41
  Alaria Soup, 87–88
  Apple Salad, 106
  with Beach Peas, 103
  with Clams, 91–92
  with Crabmeat, 62, 65–66
  Fish Cakes, 48–49
  Fish Stock (Court Bouillon), 54
  Gelled Tomato Salad, 81
  Irish Moss Soup, 83
  Kelp Stew, 88–89
  Mediterranean-style Sopa de Pescado, 55
  Mexican-style Fish Stew, 59
  New England Fish Chowder, 56
  as Potherb, 100, 108
  Sautéed Apples and Onions, 105
  Scallop Sauté, 71
  in Spaghetti Sauces, 75, 77–78
  Spring Stew, 96
  Steamed Mussels, 73
  Steamed Pollack, 47
  Summer Bounty Salad, 102
Beach Peas (*Lathyrus japonicus*), 31, 35, 40–41
  Alaria Soup, 87–88
  Boiled, 103
  Dried Beach-Pea Soup, 109
  Spring Stew, 96
  Stir-fried Beach Pea Pods and Mushrooms, 99
Blackberries (*Rubus*), 37–38, 104
Blueberries (*Vaccinium augustifolium*), 37, 104
Bladderwrack. *See* Rockweed
Blue Mussel. *See* Mussel
Boats, 3; launching and rentals, 120
Campgrounds, 120
Carregeenan. *See* Irish Moss
Chickweed (*Stellaria media*), 28, 32, 40–41, 94
  as Potherb, 100, 108
  Summer Bounty Salad, 102
  Wild Greens Salad, 95

Clams (*Mya arenaria*), 2
  Chowder, Quick, 91–92
  Dip, 91
  Fritters, 92–93
  Leftover Clam Meat, 91
  Newburg, 93
  Steamed, 90–91

Clover. *See* Red Clover

Court Bouillon, 54–55

Crab, Rock (*Cancer irroratus*), 11, 13–14
  Crab Cakes, 66–67
  Crabmeat Salad, 63
  Crabmeat Spread, 62
  Pure and Simple Crab, 62
  Steamed, 14

Cunner (*Tautogolabrus adspersus*), 6
  Baked in Wine, Milk, or Tomato Juice, 46
  Basic Fish Stock (Court Bouillon), 54
  Fish Cakes, 48–49
  Fish Stew, 58
  Fried, 45
  Mediterranean-style Sopa de Pescado, 55–56
  Mexican-style Fish Stew, 59
  New England Fish Chowder, 56
  Salad, 48
  Seviche, 60
  Steamed, 14

Curled Dock (*Rumex crispus*), 30, 40–41, 94
  Cheese Sauce, 98
  Creamed, 97–98
  Greens and Potatoes, 95–96
  as Potherb, 108
  Spring Stew, 96
  Wild Greens Salad, 95

Dandelion (*Taraxacum officinale*), 26, 32, 94
  Buds, Pan-fried, 97
  Greens and Potatoes, 95–96
  Spring Stew, 96
  Wild Greens Salad, 95
Dock. *See* Curled Dock

Edible Kelp (*Alaria esculenta*), 23
  Alaria Soup, 87
  Kelp and Co. Salad, 87
  Kelp Stew, 88–89
  Midrib Munch, 87
  Stir-fried, 89–90
Fish: cleaning, 10; filleting, 10–13; Soups and chowders, 53–61, *See also* Cunner, Mackerel, Pollack
Goosetongue (*Plantago oliganthus*), 33
  Boiled, Buttered and Simple, 101
  as Potherb, 100
  Summer Bounty Salad, 102
Green Sea Urchin. *See* Sea Urchin
Harbor Pollack. *See* Pollack

Irish Moss (*Chondrus crispus*), 21–22
Gelled Tomato Salad, 81–82
Hot Lemonade, 84
Puddings, 85–86
Sauce for Steamed Fish, 82–83
Soup, 83–84
Spring Stew, 96
Stir-fried, 84–85
Kelp. *See* Edible Kelp
Lamb's Quarters. *See* Seaside Lamb's Quarters
Late Summer Greens, 40–41
Fish Stew, 58
Greens and Potatoes, 95–96
as Potherb, 100
Spring Stew, 96
Wild Greens Salad, 95
Lobster (*Homarus americanus*), 2
Bisque, 70
in Clambake, 79
Newburg, 68
Quick Zesty, 69–70
Salad, 70
Steamed, 67
Stew, 68–69
Mackerel (*Scomber scombrus*), 9–10, 12–13
Baked, 52
Basic Fish Stock (Court Bouillon), 54–55
Fried, 52
Marinated and Grilled, 50–51
Mediterranean-style Sopa de Pescado, 55–56
Mexican-style Fish Stew, 59
Poached, 51
Salad, 52–53
Seviche, 60
Mint (*Mentha*), 35
Apple Salad, 106
with Beach Peas, 103
Carrots with Mint, 104
Creamed Beach Parsley, 101
Raspberry Leaf Tea, 105
Tea, 103
Mussel (*Mytilus edulis*), 16–17
Roasted, 75
Seafood Spaghetti Sauce, 75
Steamed, 73
Stewed, 74
Mustard (*Brassica nigra*), 30, 32, 100
Creamed, 97–98
Greens and Potatoes, 95–96
Mustard Blossoms in Potato Salad, 100
as Potherb, 100
Spring Greens, 94
Spring Stew, 96
Summer Bounty Salad, 102
Wild Greens Salad, 95
Nesting Islands, 120
Orach (*Atriplex patula*), 29, 32, 94
Creamed, 97–98

Parsley. *See* Beach Parsley
Peas. *See* Beach Peas
Periwinkles (*Littorinidae*), 17–18
  Marinated, 77
  Spaghetti Sauce, 77–78
  Steamed, 76
  Irish Moss Soup, 83
  Kelp and Co. Salad, 87
  Kelp Stew, 88–89
Pollack (*Pollachius virens*), 6
  Baked in Wine, Milk, or Tomato Juice, 46
  Basic Fish Stock, (Court Bouillon), 54
  Fish Cakes, 48–49
  Fish Stew, 58
  Fried, 45
  Mediterranean-style Sopa de Pescado, 55–56
  Mexican-style Fish Stew, 59
  New England Fish Chowder, 56
  Seviche, 60
Public Lands, 24
Red Clover (*Trifolium*), 36
  Tea, 104
Raspberries, (*Rubus*), 37–38, 104; leaves, 38
Red Tide, 2, 16
Rockweed (*Fucus*), 21
  in Clambake, 79
  in Fish Stock, 54
  as flavoring, 80
  with Steamed Mussels, 73
  with Steamed Pollack or Cunner, 47
  Tea, 80
Rose Hips (*Rosa rugosa*), 39–40
  Cinnamon Rose Tea, 108
  Cold Rose Hip Soup, 107
  Syrup, 108
  Tea, 107
Scallops (*Placopecten magellanicus*), 2
  Bisque, 72
  Grilled, 70
  Poached, 72
  Savory Scallop Sauté, 71
Scotch Lovage. *See* Beach Parsley
Seacoast Angelica (*Coelopleurum lucidum*), 34
Sea Rocket (*Cakile edentula*), 32–33; seed pods, 40–41
  Boiled, 100–101
  as Potherb, 100
  in sandwiches, 101
  Seed pods, plain and with apples, 109
  Summer Bounty Salad, 102
Seaside Lamb's Quarters (*Chenopodium album*), 29, 32, 40, 94
  Creamed, 97–98
  Greens and Potatoes, 95–96
  as Potherb, 100
  Spring Stew, 96
  Wild Greens Salad, 95
Seaside Plantain. *See* Goosetongue

Sea Urchin (*Strongylocentrotus drobachiensis*), 18–19
  Roasted, American Indian Style, 79
  Roe Caviar, 78
  Steamed Roe, 78
Sea Vegetables, 20
Seviche, 60
Sow Thistle (*Sonchus arvensis*), 27, 94
  Greens and Potatoes, 95–96
  as Potherb, 100
  Spring Stew, 96
  Wild Greens Salad, 95
Spring Greens, 25–31
  Creamed, 97
  Fish Stew, 58
  Greens and Potatoes, 95–96
  Irish Moss Soup, 83
  Kelp and Co. Salad, 87
  Kelp Stew, 88–89
  Mustard or Curled Dock in Cheese Sauce, 98
  Pan-fried Dandelion Buds, 97
  Stir-fried Beach Pea Pods and Mushrooms, 99
  Wild Greens Salad, 95
Strawberries (*Fragaria vesca*), 31, 99
Summer Greens, 32
  Fish Stew, 58
  Irish Moss Soup, 83
  Kelp and Co. Salad, 87
  as Potherbs, 100
  Summer Bounty Salad, 102
Tides, 3
Urchin. *See* Sea Urchin
Wax Myrtle. *See* Bayberry
Wild Apples (*Pyrus malus*), 38–39
  Salad, 106–107
  Sautéed with Onions, 105
  with Sea Rocket Seed Pods, 109
  Stewed, 106
Wild Lettuce (*Lactuca canadensis*), 27, 32, 94
  Greens and Potatoes, 95–96
  as Potherb, 100
  Spring Stew, 96